Mountain Bike So

27 selected mountain bike ri
Granada & the Sierr

First Edition 2007

Writers

Jim deBank. Sue Savege

With route contributions from; Matt Barnicott, Jim Savege, Michael Saunders, Simon Elliot

Maps by

Matt Barnicott. Chirs Havill

ISBN: 978-0-9549762-9-3

Cover photo

Route:Tello Descent. Rider: Neil Halcrow. Photograph: Sue Savege

Publisher's note

Mountain bike routes are subject to the forces of both nature and man, and can change on a day to day basis. Every effort has been made in putting together this book to check routes and ensure the accuracy of the mapping. But beware rain can wash out the trail, forest routes can come and go and rides seem to get harder or easier in direct proportion to the amount of time spent in the saddle. Make sure you are ready for your day out in the dirt and check out the latest updates on access and trail conditions at www.bike-fax.com.

Published by Bikefax Ltd. UK. www.bike-fax.com

Contents

Introduction

Sun, sea and singletrack. Forget package holidays, golfers and ex-pats hiding from the British winter, the region of Andalucia in Southern Spain has some the finest and most reliable mountain biking in Europe and has long been the destination for UK based mountain bikers seeking a brief solace from the british weather.

Gifted a fantastic climate for year round riding, cheap flights into Malaga and Granada, and plentiful affordable accomodation, the rural landscape littered with trails will make even the most jaded rider grin.

Sun drenched singletrack, blinding technical descents as well as laid back dirt-track adventures, this guide covers some of the best routes across Andalucia. We've been exploring the area for years and have used our indepth local knowledge to put together a selection of some of the best riding, from the sun and sea of the Costa del Sol to the mountains of the Sierra Nevada and Granada.

Riding in Spain, the when and the how.

All the trails in this book have one thing in common – for much of the year they are dry, dusty and hot. Just as in the UK, you need to be prepared for the climate, in this case swapping waterproofs and mud

Mountain Bike Southern Spain

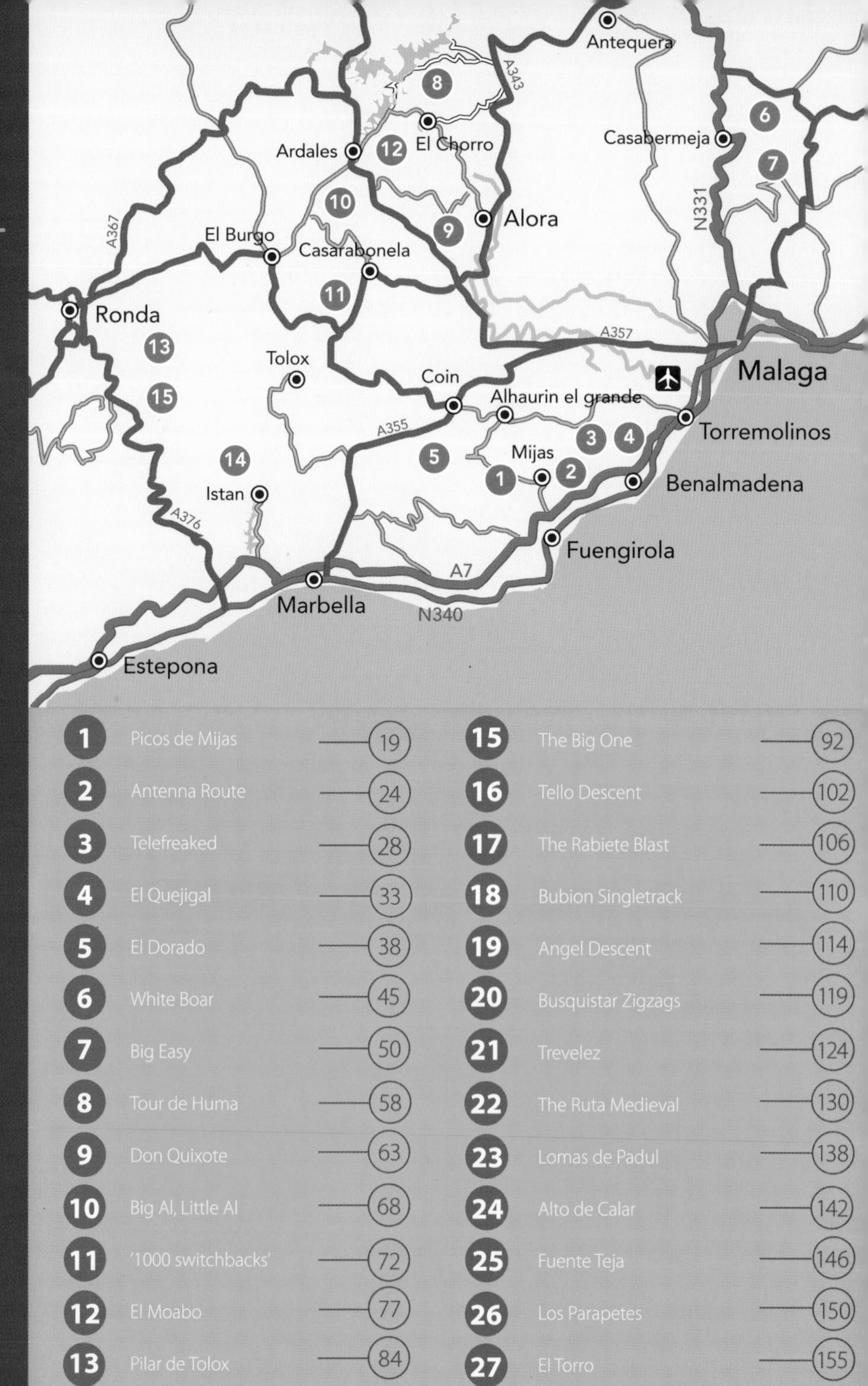

tyres for suncream, a big Camelbak and tyres able to cope with prickles, gravel and big rocks.

The climate in Southern Spain is perfect for riding for nearly all the year – the autumn and spring are deservedly the most popular with reliably good weather. A winter visit can offer a great break from the cold, dark riding to be had in northern Europe at that time of year. For the brave, or those sneaking in some summer riding, be prepared to get up early, carry a lot of water and be punished by the sun. By July and August temperatures that can easily exceed 40°C. The reward is there though – there's something great about a dawn ride, watching the sunrise over the Mediterranean and descending for breakfast and a day on the beach or by the pool.

Riding dry, dusty trails is often a novel experience for the average Brit rider! The loose surface and bare rocks demand a change in riding style to keep control – especially when a huge drop is looming from the switchbacks below you. Get your eye in by starting with one of the easier trails in the book, keep your wheels turning (locked wheels and loose surfaces don't mix!). Look for the solid sections of trail to scrub your speed and ride straight through the looser sections.

One of the things that makes the riding in Andalucia so special is how 'natural' most of it is. Lacking bermed corners and groomed trails, or the uplift of the Alps,

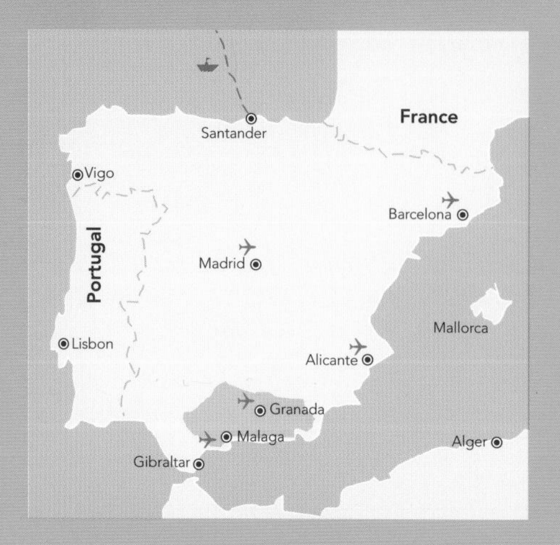

the riding here is the real deal. Expect to ride uphill, to find rocks strewn across the trail in all the wrong places and come up against impossible looking switchbacks. Experienced riders will appreciate the unique challenge, while those still serving their apprenticeship will get a fast track lesson in good technique. Relish the riding, give yourself a day or two to acclimatise to both the weather and the trails and enjoy some of the best sunshine biking around!

Whatever sort of trail you are after, DH, XC or just laid back dirt, the region has it all.

For those wanting a 'beach vacation', the Costa del Sol and the Montes de Malaga both provide stunning riding within a stone's throw of the coast. DH riders will no doubt be heading straight for the Teleferico at Benalmadena, or the rocky drops of Bubion and then on to try out the testing rocky switchbacks which are the hallmark of this region. And XC riders will just love it everywhere.

For mountain lovers, drive inland to the Sierra de las Nieves and Guadalhorce Valley and find unspoilt riding on endless trails in a 'big mountain' environment.

Or head east to the really big mountains of the Sierra Nevada and the Alpujarras where trails take on a much grander scale, with rides that easily equal the Alps in length and technicality. For those with time, the energy and a thirst for stunning trails, there's more riding in Andalucia than you can dream of. This guide can only scratch the surface of what is a true mountain biker's paradise.

Getting yourself there

With the advent of budget airlines, Spain has become one of the cheapest and most accessible places to visit in Europe. Cheap flights and low-cost car hire mean there's almost no reason to drive unless you're planning to come for a few months! Just about every airline flies into Malaga, and now with regular flights into Granada, access into the east of the region is also quick and easy.

Currently, Easyjet, Jet2.com and Monarch all fly daily into Malaga and Ryan Air has a regular service to Granada.

Once in Spain the best way to get around is to hire a car or small van as towns, villages and routes are all pretty spread out.

Getting your bike there

Getting your bike across is easy enough. Most airlines now make an extra charge for a bike, but book it in early, buy a big padded bike bag, take it across to the oversize luggage desk and it's pretty much as straightforward as that.

You'll need to do a few things to prepare your bike for the flight.

- Remove the wheels, taking the skewers

out and let some but not all the air out of the tyres

- Insert spacers into the brake calipers to stop the pistons getting squeezed together (use either the plastic spacers new bikes come with, or a wedge of cardboard)
- Remove rear mech, pad it and zip tie it to the frame
- Take the handlebars off at the stem, pad them and zip tie them to your frame
- Pad everything else with clothing, bubblewrap, etc and bag or box the whole lot up
- And finally don't forget any special tools you need to put your bike back together and a roll of tape and bunch of zipties to pack for the return journey

Where to stay

Malaga Region

Just as there are more budget flights than you can shake a stick at, there seem to be an infinite number of apartments to rent on the Costa. A few minutes on the internet will turn up loads and with a few people sharing, they're very affordable. Basing yourself anywhere between Malaga and Estepona will give you easy access along the N-340 to the start of all the western routes, and the Sierra Nevada area is only two hours drive away.

The Costa del Sol doesn't suit everyone, though. If you want to experience Spain then you are better off making a base somewhere inland. El Chorro, and the Finca la Campaña, is a perfect base both for riding and for those who want to get some rock climbing or walking in, as well as blasting some singletrack. Inland towns like Ronda give you a nice taste of the real Spain with bars, restaurants and places to stay all withing easy access to the moutains and lakes of the Malaga region.

Granada Region

For those heading across to the big mountains of the Sierra Nevada and the Alpujarras, the towns of Lanjaron, Bubion and to the north, Guejar Sierra make ideal locations for a week or two in the area.

Lanjaron is a well known spa town and host to plenty of bars, both spanish and english, and the hub of a healthy network of trails. Higher up in the mountains, the tiny whitewashed village of Bubion gives you a taste of old Spain and arguably some of the most technically challenging riding around.

Head to the northern side of the Sierra Nevada and the small town of Guejar Sierra, as yet unknown to mountain bikers, is a great base for ticking off the routes.

Andalucia is well known on the outdoor tourism circuit and any quick web search will turn up a host of cottages, apartments and old farmhouses for rent. Hostales are also good places to stay, more upmarket than british hostels and not as chintzy as B&Bs.

In Spain you'll pay by the room for a bed, which works out pretty cheap for two sharing, and breakfast is usually just a few euros extra.

Andalucia also lends itself to road-tripping. For those travelling around, every town has at least one 'pension'; inexpensive hotels perfect for a few nights before you move on.

Camping is easy with many well equipped sites, often with the option of staying in tents or wooden cabins and all mod cons such as washing machines and an all important bar and restaurant.

Tourist information offices have maps of all the main campsites. If you can't find a tourist office, heading into the Ayuntamiento (Town Hall) of many of the smaller towns and asking will often get you a list of local accomodation (Alojamientos) and places to visit.

Where to eat

Eating in Spain is always a joy. Try 'tapas', small dishes of local cuisine, from patatas to pollo, available at every small bar and roadside cafe, or ask for 'Raciones' (a bigger version of tapas) if you are hungry The best way to eat when travelling in Spain is to stop at a Venta, little bar/restaurants at the side of every road, and have the Menu del Dia. These menus are fantastic value, usually with three courses plus a drink for under €10, just don't expect to get on your bike afterwards! But as a finish to a big morning ride, this is the way to eat, just turn up at 2pm and fill your belly.

And if you cant bear to part with your ata British food, don't worry, this area has more than its fair share of English pubs and cafes, and English speaking waiters.

Bike shops

Spanish bike shops are a trip back in time for UK riders, and usually resemble more of a cycle hardware shop than bike boutique! Though usually well stocked and friendly, they are rarely near to the riding areas so it's always a good idea to bring basic spares with you unless you fancy half a day driving to a bike shop for a few tubes

Malaga Ciclo Hobby, Calle Lope de Rueda 127 – 131, Puerto de la Torre. www.ciclohobby.es

Coin Autorecambios Cecilio, Bloque la Palmera, Avda Reina Sofia

Marbella Bike Station Marbella, C. Nuestra Señora de Gracia 28. www.bikemarbella.com

Torremolinos Xtrem Bike, Avda. Las Mercedes, 14. 29620 Torremolinos 0034 952 380 691

xtremebike@teleline.de

Granada Semar Elite, San Anton 83, 18005 0034 958 251 862 semarelite@semarelite.com

Weather

Despite the fantastic climate, the Spanish are as obsessed about the weather as everyone else, complaining like the best of them if it's too wet, too dry, too hot or too cold (cold here, though, means anything less than 15C!). Although it can be cool in the mountains, it's pretty rare to need long pants, though longsleeves, though a windproof are always useful. From mid June to early September, the weather is 'scorchio' and the TV weather forecasts have more than a passing resemblance to the Fast Show sketch.

Forecasts are easily obtainable: most bars and cafes have TVs permanently on and weather forecasts are regular on each channel. The local daily paper for region, Sur, has weather maps and is often to be found at the end of the bar in cafes.

For those with web access, www.inm.es, the Spanish Met office, is as accurate as any and will also provide fairly specific area forecasts as well as general forecasts, satellite pictures etc. Global Radio (96.5 FM), an english language channel has regular forecasts.

A quick note about the climate

The reason why everyone comes to Andalucia

is the weather, but this far south the sun is strong all year round. Shades and suncream are a must, as is plenty of water on the trail. In the summer, temperatures can easily reach 40°C, so an early start, a generous dollop of suncream and plenty of liquids are a must in order to enjoy the riding. There are plenty of natural springs, known as 'fuentes' and these real lifesavers are generally marked on the maps.

From November to April, it still possible to get caught out in rain showers and snow can fall on the higher mountains so at this time of year it's advisable to carry a shell jacket, as well as your factor 30.

How to use this guide

We all know how difficult it is to turn up in a brand new area, not knowing quite where to start, hence this guide. With the help of local riders, we've done some of the work for you, checking out the local services and riding the trails with notebook, camera and GPS, to put together the best information possible.

To make it easy for riders to choose the right route, the routes have been arranged by geographic area, with each area then giving a selection of routes at a variety of grades. If you want to find all the downhill, cross country, epics etc in the region, have a look at the 'Graded List' at the back of the book.

Maps & symbols

The maps used in this guide are based on standard local mapping. The maps have then been redrawn to highlight the most important information whilst giving mountain bike riders additional detail to help with getting the most out of the ride.

Whilst we have made every effort to check the accuracy of our maps, there are times when only a full detailed map will do and for the longer, more remote rides we strongly recommend that you take a map and compass with you and know how to use them.

Icons

The icons on the map give you extra information about the nature of the trail, as well as the location of any amenities such as bike shops and cafes etc.

Gradings explained

The gradings in this book are here for you to decide what's your own poison: ride with the challenge of never 'dabbing'; push yourself on something a little harder than usual, or stay well within your comfort zone.

It is notoriously hard to grade the level of difficulty of mountain bike routes. So much will depend on you, the bike and the conditions on the day. As well as this, the level of difficulty of a route can change by the day, as tracks get worn out, maintained or rebuilt. In this book we attempt to give you some guide as to the level of the hardest riding to expect on each route. Remember though it is only a guide.

Downhill routes - DH

Where possible, we've indicated which routes are suitable for DH riders. These routes mean that usually you'll either have to sort a lift out or be prepared for a spot of pushing.

Downhill routes are given a technical grade from 1 to 5 to indicate their level of severity and technical difficulty. The higher the grade: the harder the route. All this means higher grades equal bigger jumps, steeper inclines and more demanding technical sections.

1 Easy

Straightforward off-road riding, mainly on forest roads and wide grassy tracks. All you need is some knobbly tyres on your bike and you can go for it. Suitable for all including novices and children.

2 Moderate

Wide bumpy trails, simple singletrack, moderate inclines and nothing too technical.

3 Hard

Fast flowing singletrack, with generally good traction on the surface. Good bike control needed and some quick decision making. Expect variable surfaces from smooth hardpack to loose rock, mud and roots and small jumps

4 Extreme

Technically challenging riding with tight switchbacks, narrow rutted tracks and loose surfaces. Fast riding with jumps, steep inclines and obstacles all around you. Riding where expert bike control is essential and good balance at a premium. On DH tracks at least wear elbow and shin pads for protection.

5 Off the Scale

Big jumps, scary landings, impossible surfaces and split second decision making. You'll most likely be wearing full body armour for this stuff. Limited or no chicken runs here. Routes for those who 'have it' on a regular or competition basis. If you don't find these rides hard – turn pro!

Cross country rides - XC

Cross Country rides use a dual grading system to indicate both the nature of the ride and the hardest level of technical difficulty which you are likely to encounter.

First of all the overall grades, here ranging from 'Epic to Blast', give you a general impression of the route, then numeric 1 – 5 grades, give you an idea of the technical difficulty of the ride. Put the two gradings together, for example, 'Expert 3" to get the real impression what to expect on a cross country ride.

Epic

Epic routes, as the name implies, can contain serious sections of downhill for long periods of time, or thigh-ripping technical uphill, or both! These rides will present some severe endurance issues! Go prepared as anything can come at you at anytime.

Expert

Almost wholly off-road. You'll need a reasonable level of fitness and a fair bit of experience on a bike. Riding on these trails can be of a challenging nature and you'll be trying your best not to fall off.

Classic

With big sweeping views and good distance, these rides can take you far from the beaten track. Classic routes will appeal to the rider who wants to cover the miles, see the scenery.

Blasts

Blow away the cobwebs when you've only got an hour or so to spare or for when the weather is being particularly ugly in the mountains. These routes offer a quick up and down, but don't underestimate them, some of these little routes can pack a powerful punch.

Kit and equipment

Going off the beaten track or into the high mountains in Spain can easily mean not encountering any towns, villages or people all day! That's the beauty of this region, but it is also all the more reason to be totally self sufficient by carrying a few extra bits with you.

- Spare food & clothing
- First Aid kit
- Hydration
- Couple of spare tubes each
- Repair kit/Multi-tool & chain tool
- Zip ties & gaffer tape (you can temporarily fix just about anything with these)
- Mobile phone - be aware that you may not be able to get a signal in some places
- A well maintained bike
- Local map and GPS if you've got one

Downhill (DH)

Downhill riding in Spain is pretty steep and stoney. Coupled with this, end up off your bike and if you don't hit the rocks, you'll end up in the prickly bushes on the side of the trail, so we recommend that you pad yourself up well.

- Full gloves
- Full face helmet (never go on DH trails without at least a normal MTB helmet)
- Long sleeves
- Full body armour if you've got it
- Elbow guards
- Knee and shin pads at least
- Chainguard (to protect your bike)
- Spare brake pads

Very useful spanish words

Acequia	Irrigation canal
Bici/Bicicleta	Bike
Cañada	Drovers road
Cerro	Hill
Collado	Mountain pass
Cerveza	Beer
Cortijo	Farmhouse
Claro	OK
BTT	MTB
Derecha	Right
Embalse	Reservoir
Fuente	Water fountain
Izquierda	Left
Mierda!	oh shit...!
Pista	Wide dirt track
Rio/barranco	River
Senda/Sendero	Path
Venta	Roadside bar
Inner Tube	Camara
Tyre	Cubierta
Brake Pads	Zapatas
Lube	Lubricante
Chain	Cadena
Puncture repair kit	Parches
Rear Mech	Cambio
Front Mech	Desviador
Mech hanger	Paton
Spoke	Radio
Hub	Buje
Do you have a..?	Tiene un/una..?

Special spanish kit

Bike Kit

Spanish riding is often loose and rocky. It's not unusual to bend a hanger or wear out the brake pads, so its worth packing your own spares. If you do find yourself needing to get a few things locally, it is often a good idea to take the broken bit with you to the shop to make yourself understood.

Have a look opposite for some useful spanish words and phrases to help you get by in the local shops

Personal Kit

- Sun shades
- Loads 'a suncream
- Large capacity water carrier
- Lightweight shell jacket
- And don't even consider riding here without a helmet

Code of conduct

You're not going to bump into too many people on these trails, but as most of the routes are shared with ramblers, locals, farmers and goats, it pays to be alert and be ready to give way if needs be. A goat, a bike and a rider can make a nasty mess on the trail!

- Always ride on legal trails
- Leave no trace
- Be sensitive to the soil beneath you and practice low-impact cycling.
- Stay in control of your bike
- Always give way to faster riders on DH. On XC give way to riders coming up the hill.
- Let your fellow trail users know you're coming. Anticipate other trail users around corners or in blind spots
- Never scare animals

What to do in an emergency

If it does all go horribly wrong and someone in your group ends up in a big bloody pile on the floor, first of all make sure your casualty and everyone else for that matter stays cool and comfortable, and get him or her in to shelter and patch 'em up if you can.

If they're too broken to walk out, it's probably time to call for some help. 112 is the general emergency number. 061, for ambulance services, 062 is for the Guardia Civil who operate a limited Mountain Rescue service in some areas but don't rely on a rescue service as you'd find in the UK or the Alps.

Keep the phone on, as they will need to get back to you for more details. It may then be a couple of hours before help gets to you.

For the walking wounded, most reasonable sized villages have a doctor's surgery (Centro de Salud) or an emergency room for minor injuries, 'Urgencias'. Carry your passport, E1-11 and insurance documents with you at all times to prevent paperwork nightmares.

Local Hospitals with A&E Departments

Malaga: Hospital Clinico Virgen de la Victoria, San Juan Bocso 41, 29014. Malaga. 952 256 150, just off the N357/N340.
Ronda: Hospital Oeste de - Ctra. El Burgo km 1, Ronda
Granada: 'El Cinico', Avda Dr Oloriz No 16, 18012 Granada. 958 023 000

The moral of the story is RIDE SAFE, take plenty of kit and 'don't crash and burn'.

Trail access in Spain

For many years Spain has had a slightly anarchic attitude to the use of footpaths and trails around the countryside. Nowadays however the same pressures that are being felt everywhere by the sheer number of trail users, means that a degree of organisation and legislation is coming into play regarding mountain bike trails.

Just like France, Spain now has a growing number of waymarked trails for mountain bikes. But whilst these trails are proliferating up in the North East of Spain, they have yet to hit the scene in Southern Spain.

Many of the mountain bike trails in this guide follow GR (Gran Recorridos) paths. These are long distance paths that cross the whole of Europe, and the GR7 in the Sierra Nevada has some particularly challenging riding. GR's are waymarked with red and white stripes on wooden posts with occasional signposts.

PR (Pequeno Recorridos) are local versions of the GR's and are usually well maintained and waymarded by the local authorities. These are waymarked with yellow and white stripes on wooden marker posts.

Both GR and PR trails are multi use, and you as likely to see walkers on them as you are to see goats and horse riders. These trails can get very busy in the summer holidays, so you will need to keep your eyes peeled and be ready to slow down at all times.

There is no way of telling on Spanish maps what is a public right of way and what is not, and if you are going off exploring by yourselves you might encounter the odd trail with a chain across it, a no entry sign or even a feisty local. Unfortunately we've got to the end of many fine pieces of trail, to find exactly this situation. There's nothing you can do about it other than politely leave, preserving both your and the mountain bike community's dignity.

In the Sierra Nevada National Park mountain biking is only allowed on the fire-roads and is forbidden above 2000m. This is by and large to preserve the lives of mountain bikers, as the mountains here go up to 3,800m and both the altitude and the weather can be killers. Just recently the park wardens have taken to spot fining people who break this rule!

Finding your way

On the road

The Spanish road network seems to be in a constant state of flux. On the Costa, new buildings, golf complex's and even whole villages seem to spring up out of nowhere. Major European investment in the main transport networks for the whole country means that complete new roads and motorways may not even be mentioned on the maps.

An in-car Sat Nav system is invaluable in Spain. The Spanish are quick and decisive drivers, fair but always in a hurry. As well as this, slip-roads are short and turn off signs are usually situated immediately before the turn off, making exits easily missed. In the mountains, with less roads and less drivers, navigation is more straightforward, but even if it's just for use to get yourself out of the city, if you've got a portable Sat Nav system, take it with you. You'll find that next to your bike, it will be your best friend for a week.

On the trail

Whilst we do our best to supply you with as much route information as possible,

dirt
mountainbike
magazine
dolce ti
AS-R
FOX

it is inevitable that at some point, either concentration is going to lapse, or something is going to change on the trail and suddenly you're not quite sure where you are.

Out in Spain we've found a GPS an invaluable tool on XC rides. Coupled with a local map, it can help you get you on the right track again, or loaded up with the track from your Bikefax i-guide, should be able to keep you on the straight and narrow all the way.

Setting up your GPS for Spain

You will need to set up your GPS to work on Spanish grid and datum. To do this follow these simple steps:

- Turn the GPS. Go to the Main Menu
- Choose 'Set Up'
- In Set Up go to 'Location Format'
- In Location Format, choose 'UTM
- Set the Map Datum
- In Map Datum choose 'European 1950
- If asked for map zone, type in '30S

Once this is done, the grid references you get displayed on your GPS will correspond with the grid references displayed along the top and sides of the local maps.

To display your tracks correctly on the computer you will also need to input the location format and datum. This can usually be found in 'Preferences'.

Maps & guidebooks

For most of the Malaga Region, the best maps to use are the IGN 1:25,000 series and sheet numbers and titles are included in each area and route description. Many of the Natural Parks, such as the Sierra de las Nieves have their own specific maps. The Sierra Nevada, conveniently for us, is covered in the main by just one map.

Tracking down maps in Spain is far more tricky than getting them in the UK, so it pays to spend a few minutes on line and get your maps ahead of time. You can buy maps on line from :

www.bike-fax.com
www.cordee.co.uk
www.tiendaverde.es
www.mapasycia.com

In Spain maps for the Malaga Region can be bought in the very freindly and English speaking shop; 'Mapas y Campana on Calle Fajado 4, Plaza de la Constitution in Malaga.

The Sierra Nevada map (1:40,000 Series Alpina) is easy to get hold of once you are in the area. Here you will find them in most bookshops in and in the petrol station at Pampaneira.

The 'Trailrider Guide' which covers the whole of Spain is also a very useful resourse for the area and has loads of ideas for other places to go on future trips. www.trailriderguide.com

Digital mapping for Spain

You can view the routes digitally with a few different programmes. You can view tracks from Bikefax CD-ROM's or i-guides with any of these programmes.

To view the GPS tracks you can subscribe to Google Earth Plus. Compegps is a nice user friendly programme, and you can buy digital maps for most parts of the world, or scan your own in. GPSUtility is a free basic gps track management system, which allows you to view gps tracks and to scan in and calibrate your own maps to overlay tracks on.

Section 1

Pico de Mijas	 01	XC
Antenna Route	 02	XC
Telefreaked	03	XC / DH
El Quejigal	 04	XC / DH
El Dorado	 05	XC

Introduction

Just behind the coastal strip lies an unlikely mountain bike playground. The peaks and ridges above the Costa de Sol have a surprisingly 'big mountain' feel about them and you're unlikely to see many other people on any of the trails once you leave the honeypot of the cablecar station at Benalmadena.

Routes here are never easy and range from the perfect natural singletrack of the Pico de Mijas to the area's only purpose built downhill course at Benalmadena. The unique combination of sand and rocks on the trails make for some amusing 'sideways moments'.

A couple of the rides are perfect for quick blasts if you can only grab a couple of hours away from the apartment, family and pool. Use the Telefrico in Benalmadena for quick upward access to the 769m summit of Calamoro.

At Benalmadena, there are both XC and DH routes to play on. Though the DH tracks are not yet quite the groomed trails of Morzine or Les Gets. There's fun to be had in the Mijas forest where purpose built trails are emerging and are well worth an afternoon session.

The other routes are longer XC adventures and will take you far from the hubbub and reward you with views south to the Mediterranean, east to the distant snowy peaks of Sierra Nevada and north to glimpse the mountains covered in the rest of this guide.

Getting there

For those staying on the coast, the main coast road – the N340 – provides the access to all the routes in this section. Leave the motorway at km 217 (Benalmadena – Arroyo de la Miel) for the Cablecar and El Quejigale routes and km 222 (Mijas) for the other routes in the area.

The Teleferico at Benalmadena

Located next to Tivoli World in Benalmadena, the cablecar is clearly visible as it crosses the N340 and provides access to the summit of Calamoro. Open from mid Feb to the end of December each year. At the time of writing, a single journey costs €6.50 while a season pass valid for the whole year was €49. A bargain as this covers all the amusements at the Selvo Parks to be found all along the coast. You'll need to remove your front wheel to get it in the gondola, so take the appropriate tools

To drive to the lower cablecar station from the N340, take the exit for Benalmadena (Arroyo de la Miel at km 217) and follow the signs. For more info: www.teleferico.com,

tel: 902 19 04 82

Food and drink

Benalmadena and the Costa has a huge choice of places to eat. From Chinese, Thai, Indian, Italian and even Spanish food, no one will go hungry.

Further inland, Mijas has a good range of (slightly touristy) cafes for refuelling. The Venta los Morenos (closed Thursdays) is a useful place to stop just off the Mijas Singletrack route. Finca la Mota is another option for food and drinks in an ex-pat kind of way. Find them both close to the BP garage at the roundabout near to Alhaurin Golf.

Summary

The route with the 'character building' climb! Once the climb is over, though, the wooded earthy singletrack just goes on forever and ever. Undulating and fast, you'd think the path had been purpose built for two wheels. Later on it really has, with one of the few purpose built XC trails in the region.

The trail takes a high level line above Mijas, with sea and mountain views before you, later joining the 'Jose Briales – El Pantera' MTB circuit and finally heading back along yet more swooping singletrack. Testing rocky sections will keep you on your toes while the grins just keep on coming as the trail unfolds.

And if you're staying nearby and have time to spare, then this wooded hillside just begs to be explored. It's just a matter of piecing all those great little sections together.

Venta los Condos
Mijas 

Expert 

Difficulty 

24 km 

600 m 

3 hrs 

Alhaurin el Grande
Coin 

Getting there

From Malaga and the coast

Park at the Venta los Condes, 6.5km from Mijas toward Alhaurin El Grande on the A-387. Reach this from Malaga and the coast via the N-340 junction at KM marker 217 (Mijas). Follow the road almost all the way into Mijas. At the roundabout just before Mijas Puelbo, turn right for Alhaurin El Grande.

From Fuengirola, the west

Take the MA426 Mijas road from the N340.

From inland areas

Head toward Alhaurin El Grande then take the road heading south from the town signposted Mijas and Fuengirola. Take the third exit at the roundabout, heading toward Mijas and passing Alhaurin Golf. The Venta is 4km from the roundabout on the left.

Start point

Leave your car at the parking opposite the Venta – or close by - and set off toward Alhaurin el Grande (pointing away from the sea).

600m
500m
400m
300m

0km
5km
10km
15km
20km
25km

Date
Time

Route description

1 Alta Verde

A quick tarmac section takes you to the KM 12 marker at Alta Verde. Turn off the road taking the track uphill until a pylon. Turn right and head around the 'Helter Skelter Hill' until you reach a junction in a clump of trees. Point your bike left and follow the dirt track.

2 Hidden turning

After a few twists and turns the track makes a sharp left hand turn downhill (about 1.6kms from joining the dirt track). Up and to your right is a trail heading up a steep slope. Gain the singletrack above and follow it upwards – the initial slog is well worth it!

3 The top

Character now firmly built, continue on the obvious singletrack ignoring the minor tracks leading off. Take care of the 'Ravine Corners' - each requires a combination of technique and a little speed to get you down and up the other side without a tumble.

4 Dirt track

Back onto dirt track. Eventually – how great was that last bit? – you come out onto another dirt track. Turn left (downhill), passing the chain, until you get to a T junction with a strange rusty metal lump.

5 Cylinder T-junction

Remember this spot. If time is short you can drop straight into the Baby's Head Ravine and the Big Dipper (see WP 10), otherwise bear right, down past the two white buildings, and turn up and right after the row of shacks. Climb sharply at first then cruise along the track, passing under some pylons until you get to a widening in the track at a firebreak with a small white sign up in the trees on your right saying 'Circuito MTB Jose Brailes "El Pantera"'.

6 MTB loop

Just opposite the sign (downhill to the west

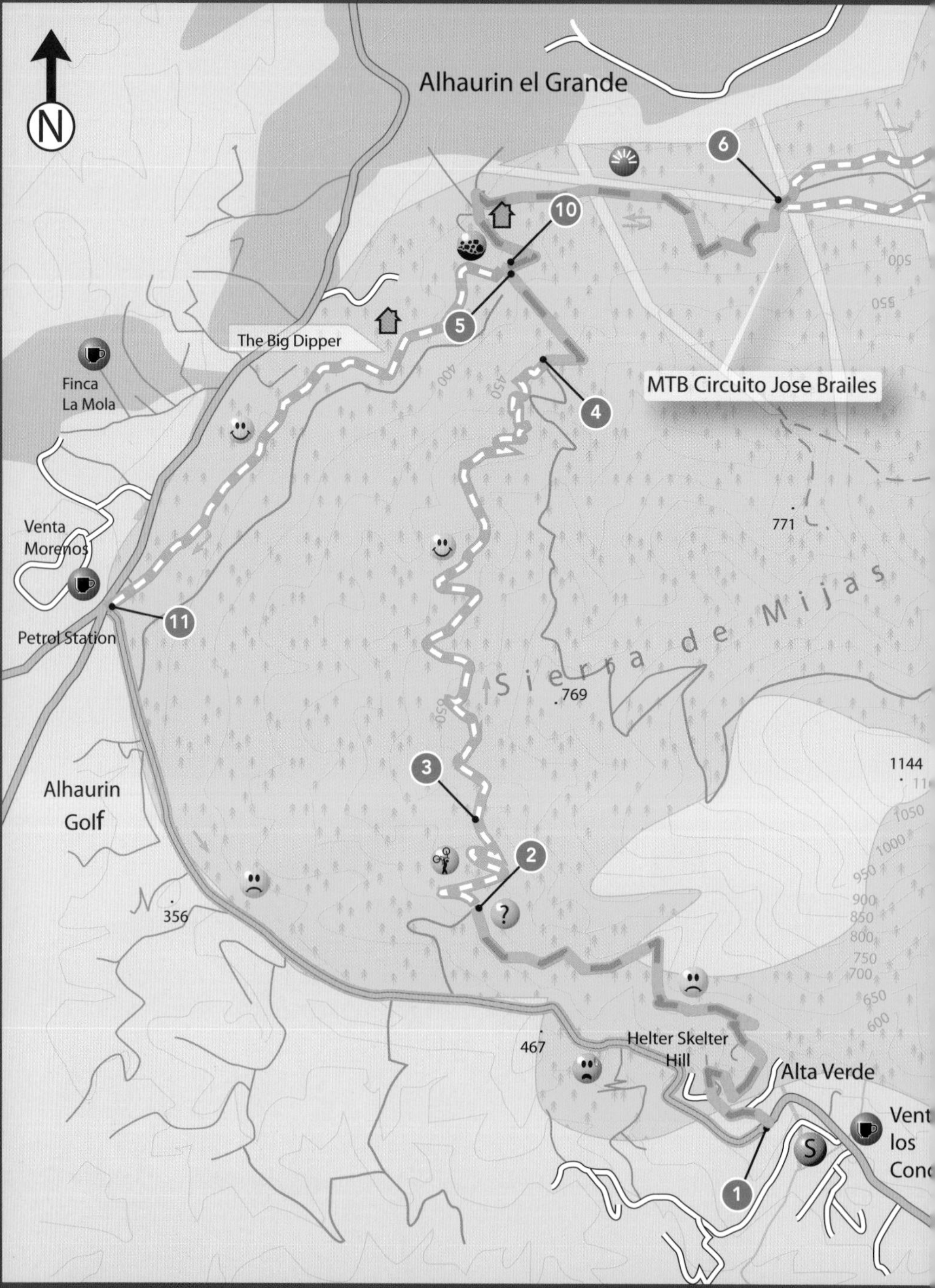

N
Alhaurin el Grande
6
10
5
4
The Big Dipper
Finca
La Mola
MTB Circuito Jose Brailes
771
Venta
Morenos
Sierra de Mijas
11
Petrol Station
769
3
1144
Alhaurin
Golf
2
356
467
Helter Skelter
Hill
Alta Verde
Vent
los
Con
1
S
400
450
500
550
650
1050
1000
950
900
850
800
750
700
650
600

of the firebreak) a thin singletrack twists in amongst trees and rocks, crossing another fire break until it runs out and reappears on the main track.

7 Fire road to Fuente Acebuche

Turn left and head along the dirt track passing through open sections with almond trees as it gains height. Ignore a couple of side turnings and keep on uphill. At the top of a stiff climb, a narrow track heads 30m uphill into the trees to Fuente Acebuche – a great place to stop and cool off.

8 The scenic dirt track.

Return to the track and carry on round, making the most of the views over the trees to the valley and the Sierra de las Nieves beyond.

9 Three way junction

A little further on, our track splits into three. Take the middle way which soon becomes a testing section of descending singletrack at the firebreak. Head gradually downwards until you reach the dirt track, turn left and return along the main track to the Rusty Lump.

10 Babies Head Ravine

Just past the rusty metal cylinder of Waypoint 5, a trail drops into the Baby's Head Ravine. Follow the trail carefully down over 'babies head' rocks until it eventally climbs steeply up and left out of the valley and continues with more forest singletrack until you get to a fire break. Cross straight over and cruise the last section of narrow floaty trail.

11 Petrol station

At the road by the petrol station, turn left and follow the road back to the start.

Summary

Short and very sweet! Take this ride as a perfect quick blast or combine it with the Mijas Singletrack route to make a really full day's riding. A nice way to enjoy this technical beauty is to aim to be at the top a little before sunset and blast down for beers and grins in the valley as the sun sets over Africa.

The route climbs up to the ridgeline above Mijas on tarmac until the viewpoint at the 939m summit of Cerro del Moro. Take it all in and then plummet back down on technical, rocky singletrack. Don't be put off by the road climb. The views are great with Gibraltar, Morocco and the Sierra Nevada all visible on a clear day

This airy trail is not for the faint hearted as the descent is steep, littered with rocks and huge drops to the side - typical of much of the mountain biking round here. The line though, is truly amazing. Just how we like it!

Mijas 

Expert 

Extreme 

10 km 

650 m 

2 - 3 hrs 

Alhaurin el Grande 1066-II 

Getting there

From Malaga and the coast leave the N-340 at KM marker 217 (Mijas junction), following the road almost all the way into Mijas and parking wherever you can.

From inland areas, head toward Alhaurin El Grande then take the A-387 heading south from the town signposted Mijas and Fuengirola. Take the third exit at the roundabout, heading toward Mijas and passing Alhaurin Golf. Eventually you descend to a T junction just before a roundabout. Parking is available in Mijas (turn right) or take the left (to Benalmadena) and follow the instructions below.

Start

Park in Mijas and take the road out of town signposted Benalmadena. 1km after the 'La Noria Urbanisation' and just after the municipal pool and Guardia Civil Barracks is a turning to the left on a sharp right hand bend (you could also leave a vehicle here). Head up the tarmac from here.

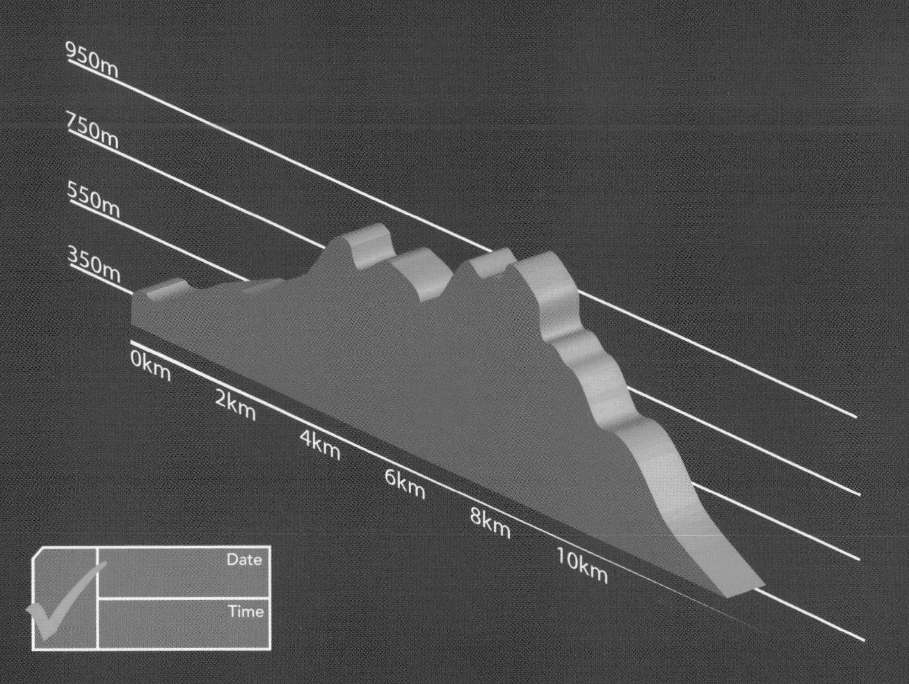

Quarry

Sierra de Don Pedro

892

745

700

650

600

500

450

1

P

BMX Park

La terraza

7

6

5

4

Mijas

Casa del Pontón

Benalmadena

600

550

500

450

400

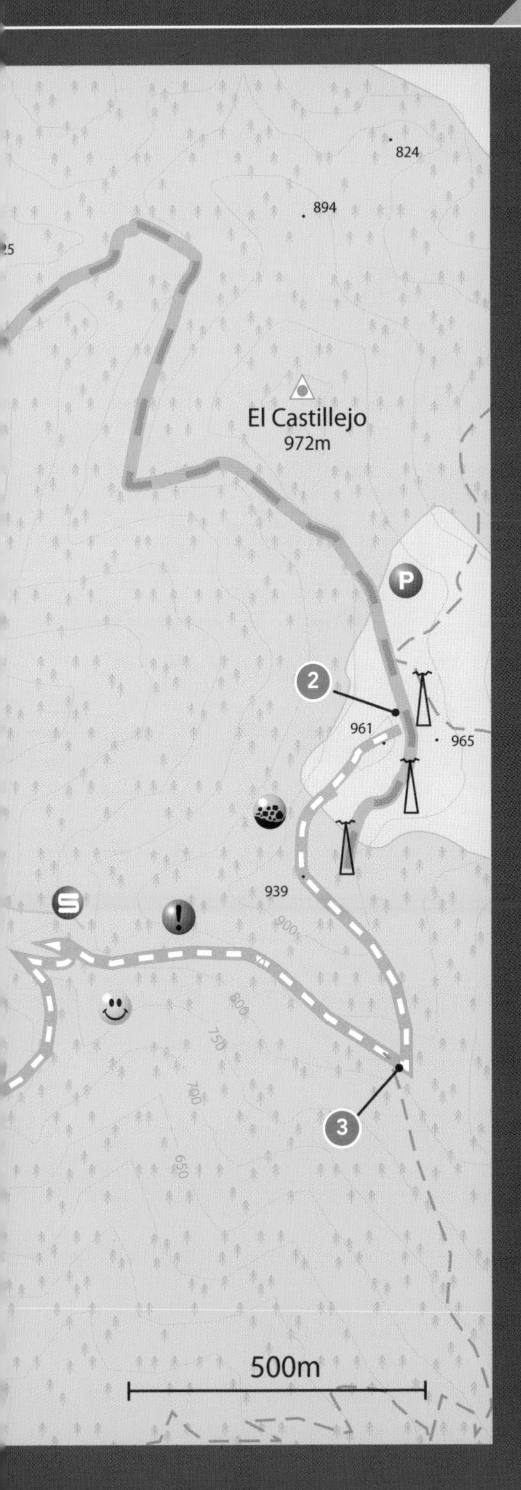

Route description

1 Parking spot road climb

Take the tarmac past the disused quarry and begin the 30min climb. Carry on all the way to the top. The descent is visible across the mountain on your right.

2 The top

Just short of the summit is a footpath on your right opposite a huge lone antenna. Take this traversing path, and continue until the first switchback junction.

3 First switchback

Follow this first switchback tightly right. Take a deep breath and get stuck in. Careful now, this is rocky death all the way!

4 T-junction

Eventually meet a path coming in from the left. Ignore it and continue downhill. After the gate you meet a surfaced track.

5 Small junction

Soon after there's another junction. Follow the switchback down and left and blast down to the riverbed below.

6 Riverbed

Cross the riverbed once then recross it keeping to the trail on the left bank of the river. After 50m, take the easy wide track up to the right and follow it to the road.

7 Main road

Turn right and follow the road for 2 mins back to your start point.

03 Costa del Sol Telefreaked

Summary

Providing the only mechanical uplift in the region, the Benalmadena Teleferico area is an almost undiscovered gem. The locals have created a couple of DH tracks and the whole hillside has loads of trails to get stuck in to. Here are a couple of options to get you started, and the rest is up to you.

The 'undertyre' surface on the top half of this trail is pretty unique, something that feels like beach sand at the top of a mountain! In places you'll be surfing. Just relax and enjoy.

Look for the map boards dotted around the mountain - a little exploration can be very rewarding around here.

The overall technical grade for this ride is 'Extreme' or you can turn into an 'Off the scale', if you go for some playtime on the DH / Freeride tracks.

Cable Car Benalmadena 

Expert 

Extreme 

15 km 

600 m 

1 - 2 hrs 

Alhaurin el Grande 1066-II 

Getting there

Leave the N-340 at KM marker 222 (Benalmadena). If you are going to use the cablecar follow the Selwo Marina signs at the first roundabout and after that the Tivoli World signs. Park at Tivoli World.

For those riding up, leave the motorway at the same junction, head under the motorway and take the left exit at the second roundabout by the petrol station. The turn off is 200m on the left but this is a 'no left turn' so carry on round the corner to another roundabout, double back on yourself and take the right turn signposted for the Cemetary. Park just past the cemetary at the dirt track on the right signposted Albergue Cañada del Lobo.

Start

There are two starts to the trails at Benalmadena, depending on whether you are having an XC or a DH day. You can start at the bottom and pedal your way up for a full XC loop, or pay your euros at the telecabine and just have a short push at the top to get you onto the trails.

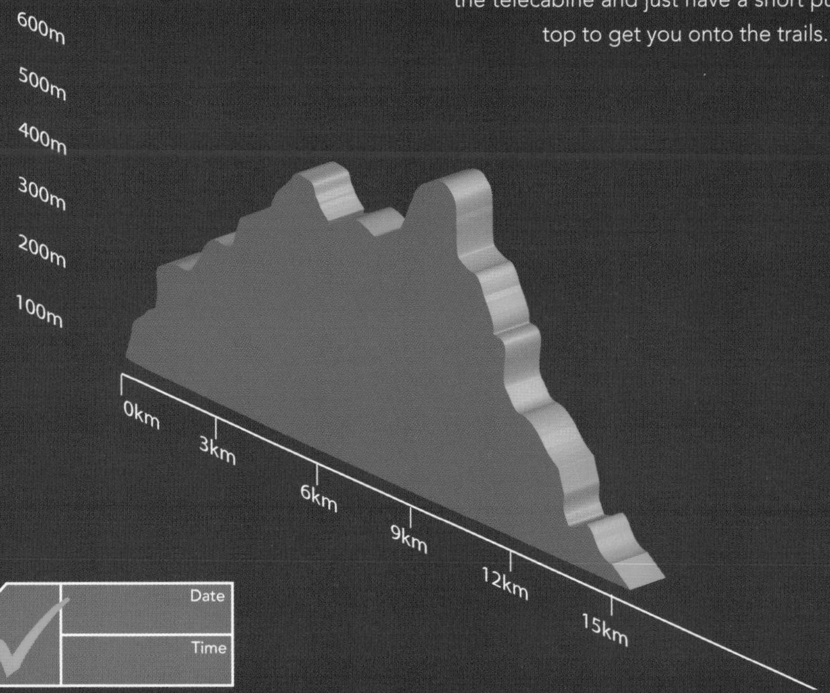

	Date
	Time

N
Quarry
Puerto de Las Ovejas
Puerto Viejo
2
3
4
5
6a
6b
7
8
1
771
369
600
550
500
450
400
350
300
250
Albergue
Cañada del
Cablecar
Downhill Tracks
Santa Angela
Monterrey
Santa Cruz
Benamania
Santangelo
Cemetery
Barrio Carola
Tivoli
P
500m

Route description

1 Parking

From the parking spot, take the tarmac track signposted to the Albergue. This becomes concrete at a disused quarry and then becomes dirt track working it's way up the valley. Persevere upwards until you get to a pass with a view into an enormous quarry and a white sign reading 'Puerto de las Ovejas' (as well as several wooden ones).

Alternatively if you want, ride on up to the cablecar station for a rest, the view and a trip to the Cafe before coming back down to the pass.

2 Puerto de las Ovejas

For the XC route, follow the trail heading westwards (on the quarry side of the hill) with the occasional steep rocky climb.

A quick way to the two DH tracks is to take the righthand trail at the Puerto and head either straight on or down to the left at the first

junction to pick up either of the jumpy bits (go to either 6a or 7 below). Shorter but sweet!

Cablecar variation

If you've taken the cablecar, leave the top station passing the Burro Stables and follow the concrete path downhill until you reach the pass of Puerto de las Ovejas, which is just after the chain across the road. Head back leftwards (to the west) on the singletrack as above.

3 Puerto Viejo

As you leave the trees, you reach a pass with lots of signposts. Take the path heading downwards toward the sea (faint blue and yellow arrows painted on rocks strewn about the trail). After 10m pass a dry fuente and seats on your right. After 100m or so the main path drops steeply. Carry on down until you reach a signposted fork in the trail.

4 Signposts

Follow the higher, lefthand path traversing the mountain, signposted very faintly 'Ermita'. After 20m fork leftwards, uphill, at the switchback. Make a rising traverse to the next ridge and cross the shoulder, descending several tricky steps as you go. Ride onwards on an increasingly good surface until you traverse above a rocky outcrop with a lone tree and map board.

5 Area de Descanso

There are two possibilities from here. Either head straight down to the right of the sign, zig-zagging until you see the blue 'Bikes only' sign marking the start of the downhill course, or altenatively you can carry on traversing round to the east.

6a Downhill Track

Full face helmet, body armour and the technical ability to match are essential here! The next km or so has a series of gap jumps, table-tops and big berms. Be brave and take them all head on or squeeze through the chicken runs to the right.

Be warned, most of the jumps aren't rollable and it's all or nothing! At the bottom you end up in a new urbanisation (under construction at time of writing). Follow your nose leftwards back to the parking spot.

Otherwise, to get back to the parking spot, follow the road downwards past the cemetery and turn right at the T-junction straight after passing under the motorway. Head to the roundabout and follow the 'Tivoli' signs and head back up for another go!

6b Singletrack option

For a less extreme singletrack descent, continue the traverse rising over another shoulder until you get to a junction with the trail coming down from Puerto de las Ovejas. This is surprisingly hard work! You'll recognise where you are if you've ridden up.

7 Switchback junction

Take the descending switchbacks and follow the trail into and down the valley. There are jumps of increasing size all the way down, most have chicken runs but don't get caught out!

8 Tarmac

Either turn right and blast downhill on the road until you get to the parking spot, or better still search out the extra bits of singletrack hiding on either side of the road.

Summary

The 'El Quejigal' ride gives the longest descent from the cablecar. With a few big drops, testy switchbacks, rocky slabs, sandy sections as well as what seems like endless undulating singletrack, this ride is guaranteed to keep you working for it. The guys who told us about this one promised a big grin at the bottom – and they weren't joking!

The loose fist sized rocks at the start can be pretty un-nerving and require a certain amount of trust and courage, but let it flow and you really can ride over them smoothly. The very first section if you ride all the way from the summit is particularly testing and steep.

The distance if you take the cable car and start at the top is 10.7km or if you ride up, 15km for the whole loop.

Getting there

Leave the N-340 at KM marker 222 (Benalmadena). If you are going to use the cablecar follow the Tivoli World signs and park there.

For those planning on riding up rather than taking the cablecar, leave the motorway at the same junction, head under the motorway and take the left exit at the second roundabout by the petrol station. Our turning is 200m on the left but this is a 'no left turn' so carry on round the corner to another roundabout, double back on yourself and take the right turn signposted for the Cemetary. Park just past the cemetary at the dirt track on the right signposted Albergue Cañada del Lobo.

Start point

Whether you are going to ride up or more sensibly take the lift, the start point is the base station for the cable car.

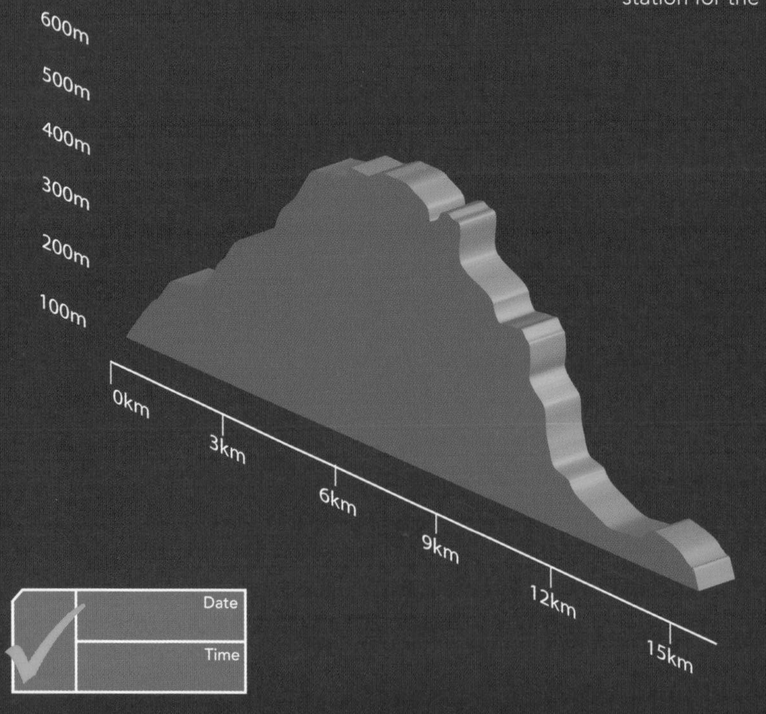

Route description

Start

Either take the cablecar to the top, leave the top station passing the 'Burros' stables and follow the concrete path up to the summit and head down from here, or follow the concrete road downhill until you reach the pass of Puerto de las Ovejas.

OR

Park the car just past the cemetery and head up the tarmac track until you reach the same pass (with the obvious sandy trail running down to your right).

At Puerto de las Ovejas, look north toward the huge Quarry and you'll see the singletrack on your left (heading west).

1 Puerto de las Ovejas

Follow the trail heading westwards, with the ocasional steep rocky climb.

2 Puerto Viejo

At the first junction, carry straight on ignoring the enticing looking trail running down left.

3 Signpost for Cerro Guerrero

Ignore the signposted trail to Cerro Guerrero, instead head up and right heading along the ridge which ends at the red and white masts at the top of the hill in front of you (which is the high point of the Antenna route).

4 Highpoint

Continue along the track until you reach a high point with a small summit to your left. Descend a little, then carry on westwards toward a main junction with three signposts and a trail heading down the valley toward to sea.

5 El Quejigal path

At the junction, turn left and begin the descent of El Quejigal. Cascade down the rocky drop offs, steep switchbacks and 'not quite pedal width' water channels and bubble over the open slabby sections as the valley walls begin to enclose around you.

6 Fuente

Traverse under the cliffs and continue on the

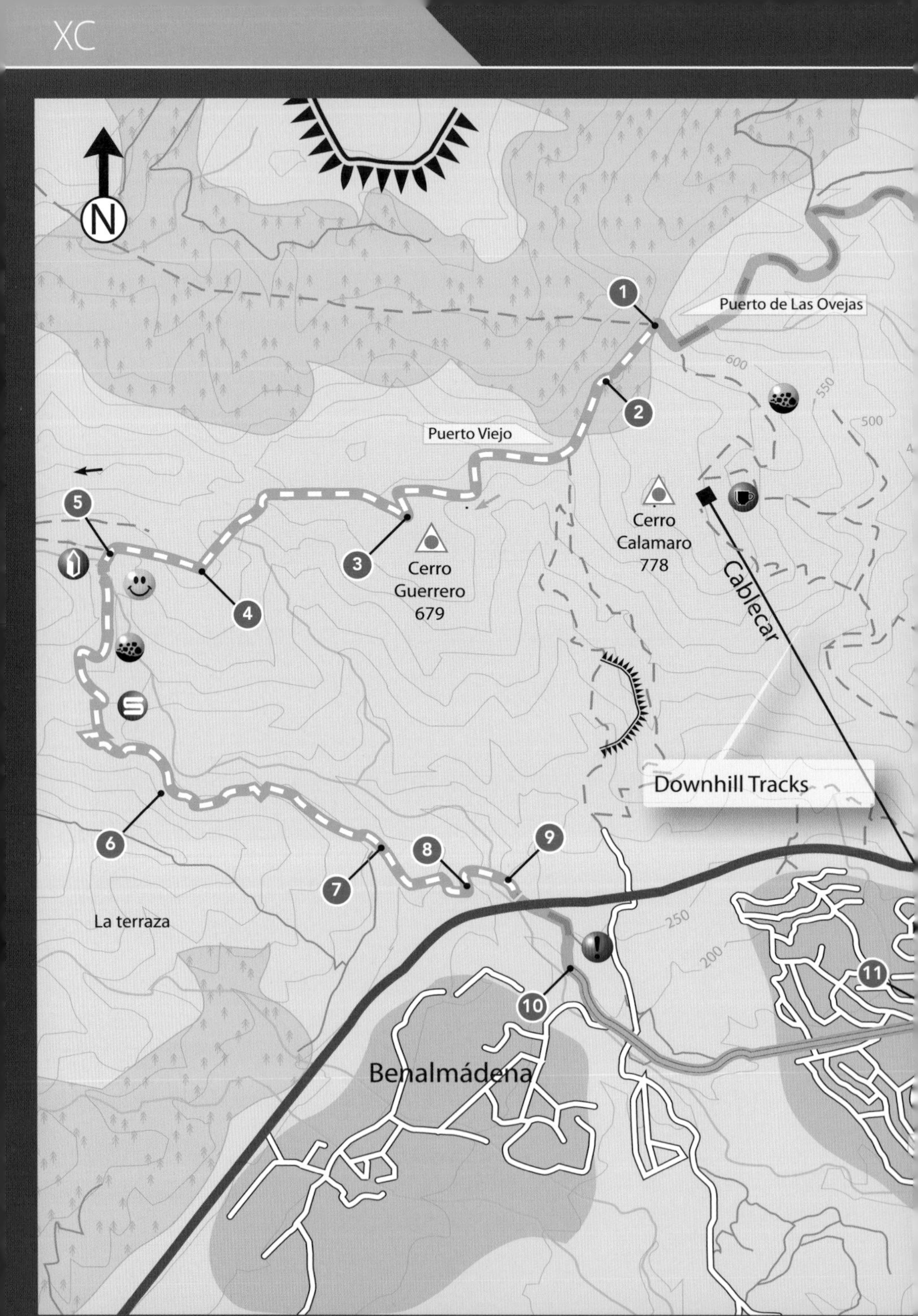
N
Puerto de Las Ovejas
600
550
500
Puerto Viejo
Cerro Calamaro 778
Cerro Guerrero 679
Cablecar
Downhill Tracks
La terraza
250
200
Benalmádena
1
2
3
4
5
6
7
8
9
10
11

trail until you cross the stream bed and make a short climb. The most technical section of the route is behind you now.

7 Junction with 'Ruta 4'

Some perfect singletrack takes you past a couple of white huts and descends through trees to a more open area. Here you'll find another signpost for the walking 'Ruta 4' Ignore it and continue on down until you come up against a pylon and the motorway.

8 Pylon

Put your grin away and descend steeply leftwards coming out near a group of huts and a dirt track.

9 Track

Ride under the motorway bridge to the road.

10 Road junction

Head left along the main road. Cruise your way upwards toward the main road, then straight across at the next roundabout.

11 Tivoli roundabout

Those who have vehicles at the cablecar station should follow the signs for Tivoli and the end of the route. To complete the loop at the cemetary parking, head straight across here (uphill). Carry on across the silver balls roundabout and again at the petrol station

12 Back to the start.

Take the left hand turn under the motorway (signposted 'Cemetario') and head back to the start.

Summary

Dale Winton aside, one the worst abominations that TV threw at us in the early 90s was the short lived soap El Dorado. Reincarnated as the Cuidad del Cine Hotel Complex, the main set for the soap still survives. The forest surrounding this is full of great riding and this route packs a lot of riding into a small area. Navigation is tricky – there are plenty of cheeky bits of singletrack diving off into the trees with no warning. Keep 'em peeled!

The first few kilometres are challenging both up and down, but after the first big fire break descent, El Dorado settles into a twisty wooded singletrack adventure linked by rocky dirt tracks and smooth flowing bits. Miss the first climb and descent and this becomes a great route to get your less experienced mates up to speed! Do the whole lot and you'll want to go round again and again.

Ciudad del Cine 

Expert 

Hard 

16 km 

600 m 

2.5 hrs 

Coin 1066-I 

Getting there

From Marbella take the main road inland toward Coin at the La Cañada shopping centre. Drive up and over, passing the village of Monda on your left. A few kms further on take the Los Llanos del Naciemiento exit.

From the Benalmadena, Fuengirola, Mijas etc, head inland toward Alhaurin El Grande and Coin. Take the left exit at the Venta los Morenos roundabout on the pass with the obvious tower (just past Alhaurin Golf). Carry on until you see signs for Los Llanos del Nacimiento and the Cuidad del Cine taking you into the forest on the right. Carry on to the Cuidad del Cine.

Inland riders should make their way to Coin and then onto the Coin bypass (A355) toward Marbella and leave the main road at the Los Llanos turn off.

600m
550m
500m
450m
400m
350m

0km 2km 4km 6km 8km 10km 12km 14km 16km

Date
Time

N
Cerro
El Gordo
629
.524
El Dorado Film Set
Coin
3km
A355
Mijas
5km
Firebreak
.448
Sports Centre
Mirador
.313
.422
.329
.341
.325
1km
1
2
3
4
5
6
7
8
9
10
11
12
13

Route description

Start

Leaving the Coin bypass at the junction marked Los Llanos de Nacimiento, follow the yellow signs into the forest taking you to the 'Cuidad del Cine' hotel complex. There is plenty of parking here.

1 Parking

Looking up at the steep fire break, a dirt track heads into the forest on your right. Take this and climb increasingly steeply past a quarry top on a sharp corner about half way up.

Near the top the track splits. Climb straight ahead towards a small col a few metres higher, ignoring the main trail heading right.

2 Saddle

At the top, choose the stoney singletrack on your left. Climb on an increasingly tricky trail keeping to the left of the rounded summit of the Cerro Gordo.

The 360° view at the top is stunning. From here you get a glimpse of all the areas covered in this section of the guide.

3 Junction

Just as you start to head down, the trail forks. Take a right here. The trail gets steeper, rockier and trickier as you descend. A couple of tight turns bring you out onto a fire break. Drop down carefully – it's steeper and looser than it looks!

4 Main track

The trail comes out onto a wide dirt track. Turn right and pedal easily on, taking the left fork when the track splits. Ride a little further until the next fire break.

As the angle eases, cross straight over the dirt track and continue downhill on the RHS of the fire break on singletrack.

5 Fire break

Turn left onto the fire break and take the initially easy singletrack heading down on the right side. It's fast and fun, but suddenly gets 'interesting' about halfway down. Take care and continue to the bottom unscathed!

6 Wooden marker post

Look to your right for a wooden marker post at the start of an uphill track. Guess what? Puff and pant up the loose rocky trail to the top.

7 Road junction

Cross over the road and follow the green signposted trail 'Al Mirador de Cerro Alaminos'. Fifty metres further on take the left fork traversing through the trees. Continue to the viewpoint where the track ends.

8 Mirador

Take a moments rest, admiring the beauty of the mountains, forests, Mediterranean, distant views of Africa and, ahem, the Costa del Sol. Double back looking for a trail dropping into the trees on your right at the first corner (about a hundred metres from the viewpoint).

Drop down to the singletrack. Fork left after only a few metres and spiral between the trees along the twisty trail. Have a 'This is why!' moment or two, following the trail downhill until you reach a fence.

Turn right, keeping the fence on your left, pedal round three sides of a square until you reach a junction.

9 End of fence

Leave the fence. and turn right on a short section of dirt track, cross the road and meander along the wide flat track until you reach the wooden marker post junction (WP 8).

Head right to cross the heathland on the obvious track running towards some floodlights on the horizon. Stop when you reach a forest of concrete based pylons and picnic spot.

10 Picnic tables

Ignoring the benches on the left of the road, head straight across towards a wooded marker post and more picnic tables on the right. The next section of singletrack starts about 5m to left of the closest table. Skim your way along the trail until you come out onto a track.

11 Track

Point your bars left and pedal uphill for a few hundred metres, stopping when the track veers left.

On your right is a steep, loose climb up a fire break. At the top look for a grafitti covered building in the trees on your right. Ride to the left hand side of it and pick up a descending concrete road.

12 Hidden singletrack

Twenty metres from the junction with the tarmac road at the bottom, is a saucy little section of trail heading back into the trees on the right. Grin your way along and cross straight over the road when you reach it. Head toward two little concrete huts and take the rising dirt track lined with wooden markers. Climb for about 250m and look out for another trail winding through the trees off to your left.

Point your trusty steed leftwards and blast along the singletrack until you reach a T-junction.

13 Dirt track

Go up and right at the junction, ascending another pebbled track toward the picnic spot. Head for the entrance to the Sports Centre and pick up the last of the singletrack running parallel to the road opposite the steps. This spits you out just short of the parking at the start. Have a cerveza at El Dorado and do another lap...

Section 2

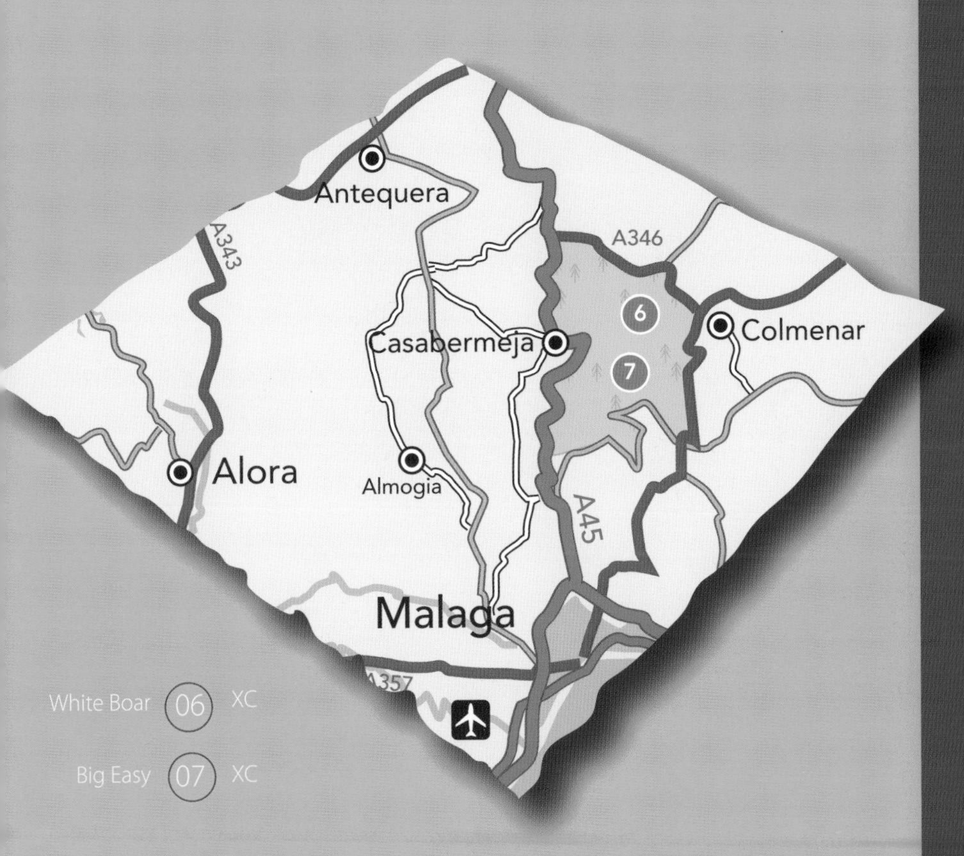

White Boar 06 XC

Big Easy 07 XC

Introduction

The least demanding of all the areas in the book, the Montes de Malaga is a huge forest area, and although it starts on the edge of the city, somehow it manages to stay a quiet forest haven teeming with wildlife.

The whole of this Natural Park is criss-crossed with forest roads. The area was deforested from the 15th Century onwards to produce timber for the Spanish Fleet, and in 1927 a huge programme of reforestation was initiated to try to control the erosion and flooding that plagued the local area as a result of the the felling.

This leaves us with a network of dirt tracks, grand cortijos in various states of repair, recently added Senderos (footpaths, or singletrack for us bikers!) and plenty of marked trails. You'll notice small coloured concrete markers all over the place, as well as coloured flashes on the trees. Each of these is a main trail through the forest. Our routes chop and change between these routes to create some fantastic riding which is big on views and more relaxed in attitude.

Bordering the city of Malaga, this is the place you're most likely to meet other bikers, both roadies making the 1000m road climb from the city, or mountain bikers of all types out for a weekend spin. Enjoy the atmosphere, and remember you're only 20mins from the biggest city in southern Spain!

Getting there

From Malaga and the west

Drive east on the N-340 (also called the A-7 and E-15) motorway toward Almeria. A little after the junction with the motorway heading north to Granada, exit the N-340 at KM marker 244 (Limonar). Take a left at the T junction passing under the bridge and another left at the roundabout to rejoin the motorway.

Leave the N-340 at KM marker 243 (Fuente Olletas and Cuidad Jardin) and head into Malaga. Just after the tunnel you'll see a junction up to the left. Take the turn-off, (small sign to Hotel C la Reina) turn left at the roundabout next to Lidls and make another left at the traffic lights onto the Camino Colmenar, the A-7000 (marked as the C-345 on some maps). Follow the winding road all the way to the start of the routes.

Food & drink

The Camino Colmenar is one of those roads used by the local Malaguenas for a weekend spin and has roadside bars dotted all the way up. There are a couple near to the Fuente de la Reina (the fuente runs for much of the year); The Venta Garvey at the start of White Boar, Venta del Mijeno and Venta El Boticario at the start of the Big Easy route and El Mirador on the horseshoe before the tunnels has spectacular views if the sky is clear and the air is clean.

Maps

The most useful map of the area is Montes de Malaga Mapa y Guia – Editorial Penebetica which comes with a small guide to walking and biking trails.

Bike shops & services

For emergency bike spares and repairs, try Ciclo Hobby (C/ Lope de Rueda, 127 – 131, Puerto de la Torre. Telephone 952 43 12 03)

Summary

A classic blast linking several sections of sublime singletrack whilst taking in the most easily accesible parts of the Montes de Malaga. Named after the unusually pale wild boar that jumped out on us while we descended the Sendero de Pocopan, you'll see plenty of trails heading off into the trees and may even spook a boar out of the scrub yourself.

The city of Malaga is often in view, but for the most part you'd never believe it was only twenty minutes away. As well as the wild boar, you'll see eagles, lizards and more local mountain bikers than you'll see anywhere else in the whole book put together!

The 'White Boar' can easily be turned into a family ride if you avoid the singletrack and stick to forest tracks.

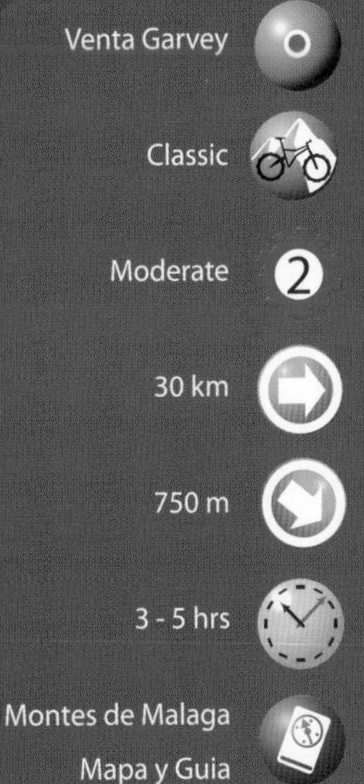

Getting there

Head up the Camino Colmenar, passing under two spiralling tunnels until you reach the Fuente de la Reina. Continue for another 5km and park at the roadside bar of the Venta Garvey.

Montes de Malaga; Mapa y Guia – Editorial Penebetica is the best map for the area, though the IGN 1053-I Los Gamez also covers the area.

Start point

Venta Garvey, 10km south of Colmenar.on the C345

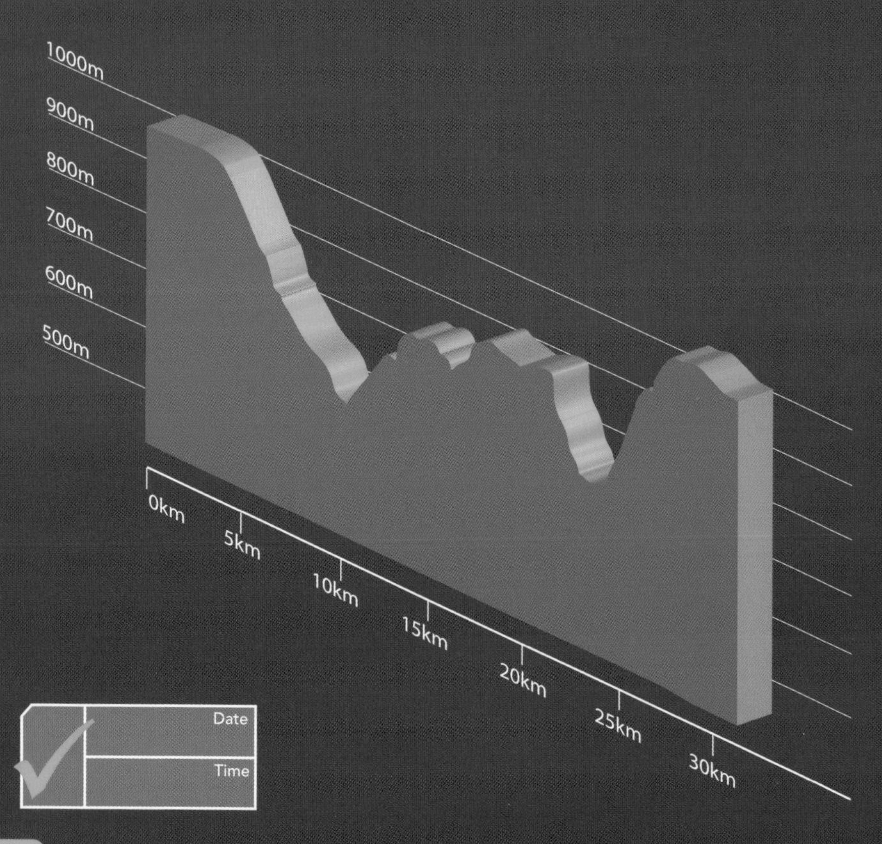

Date

Time

Route description

Start:
Venta Garvey

Head northwards along the road from the Venta Garvey, passing a small white building on your right – El Lince. Continue for a couple of kms until you see a large white sign on the wall commemorating the reforestation project of 1920's and a dirt track heading up.

1 Dirt track

Leave the road and ride uphill on the track.

2 El Lince singletrack

After 200m or so, you reach the ridge marked with a green barrier. The peak of Viento is straight ahead, but our trail doubles back left crossing the chain before following the ridge southward on swoopy singletrack. Blast down until you come out at the layby opposite El Lince.

3 Descent to Torrijos

Double back to your right at the layby on a chained forest track. Continue until you reach the firebreak.

Descend it to another track below on an indistinct path. The easiest entry and exits to the firebreak are on the right hand side as you look downwards. At the bottom, turn left onto the dirt track and follow it round to a T junction. Take a right and ride a couple of hundred metres to the map board.

4 Sendero Torrijos

From the mapboard, turn left off the main track following the sweet singletrack past the picnic spot and camping area (water here). Cross several bridges before coming out on more forest road. Carry straight on, ignoring the junction to the Mirador Martinez – Falero until you see a large ruin sprouting a palm tree on the skyline to your right. This is the Lagar de Chincilla. Start looking for the next turning on your left.

5 Chained track

Climb up the dirt track, passing the chain and continue to gain height as you traverse round the hill. Eventually, you'll reach a ruin with cedar and palm trees running wild. Take the left fork, steeply uphill and the next left at the T junction. Pass the fuente (under construction as we write this) and continue to the cross roads at the big white sign (the Monolitho de Pocopan) marking the way to Timoteo amongst others.

6 Popocan

From the Monolitho, follow the arrow and take the unchained track traversing round the right hand side of the peak.

7 Singletrack

After 1km you reach a junction with a chain dangling a 'No Entry' sign to your left. On your right is a wooden marker post; the white arrow shows you the start of the trail. Blast the singletrack, cross straight over the firebreak and continue down to Las Contadoras, an old forest building which has now been turned into a Field Study Centre.

8 Tarmac

Tarmac climb. Climb out of the valley on a good road to the next junction.

N
5
Lagar de Chincilla
6
Mirador
807
Monolitho de Popocan
7
802
8
9
Field Study Centre
Monolitho de las Contadoras
Aula de Naturaleza Las Contadores
10
12
800
700
724
Reina 1032
La Humaina Hotel
770
Mirador
11
To Malaga

9 Monolitho de las Contradoras

Pass the Monolitho (the supersized white milestone) and carry on past the Sendero Contadoras map board on your right. Take the right fork at the next junction for 'La Humanina' Hotel and descend for a short way on more tarmac.

10 Dirt track

Leave the tarmac on a minor dirtrack (chained as usual) just before a sharp left hand bend with a viewpoint up to your right. Continue all the way along, until the trail finishes at a chain and junction.

Take the right fork and continue to the Mirador del Cocino. Follow the track as it doubles back and keep your eye out for a wooden marker post in the bushes on your left.

11 Singletrack

Bear left onto the descending trail passing a couple of tricky rocky sections. Eventually you'll come out at the La Humaina Hotel. Struggle back up the tarmac to the main track at the top. Turn right toward the big red and white antenna.

12 Junction

After 1km and before the antenna, a dirtrack heads off leftwards across the firebreak. Follow it all the way, traversing round the peak of La Reina, ignoring minor forestry trails, eventually coming out at the road near to the signs for Torrijos.

13 Road

Turn left and ride the road back to the Venta Garvey.

Summary

A perfect introduction to the Montes de Malaga. Overlooking Malaga and the Mediterranean, the 'Big Easy' keeps to forest tracks all the way and is ideal for less experienced riders. Put the big climb behind you at the start and enjoy the endless downhill – just don't forget to look out for the turnings as you go!

The forest is littered with waymarked trails, all marked on the local 'Editorial Penibetica' map and with marker posts and map boards at strategic points around the forest, this is one of the few mountain biking areas around where you won't get horribly lost if you go exploring.

As well as enjoying the riding in the forest the vultures at El Boticario are definately worth a visit.

El Boticario 

Classic 

Moderate 

28.5 km 

520 m 

3 hrs 

Montes de Malaga Mapa y Guia 

Getting there

Coming from the direction of the coast leave the N-340 at Limonar and head up the Camino Colmenar (A-7000) until KM marker 24. A little further on you'll see the Ventas Mijeno and El Boticario on your right.

Start point

To your left is a large layby with a huge white arrow and the words 'Repoblations Hidrologico-Forestales del Estado' marking the way into the forest. Park here.

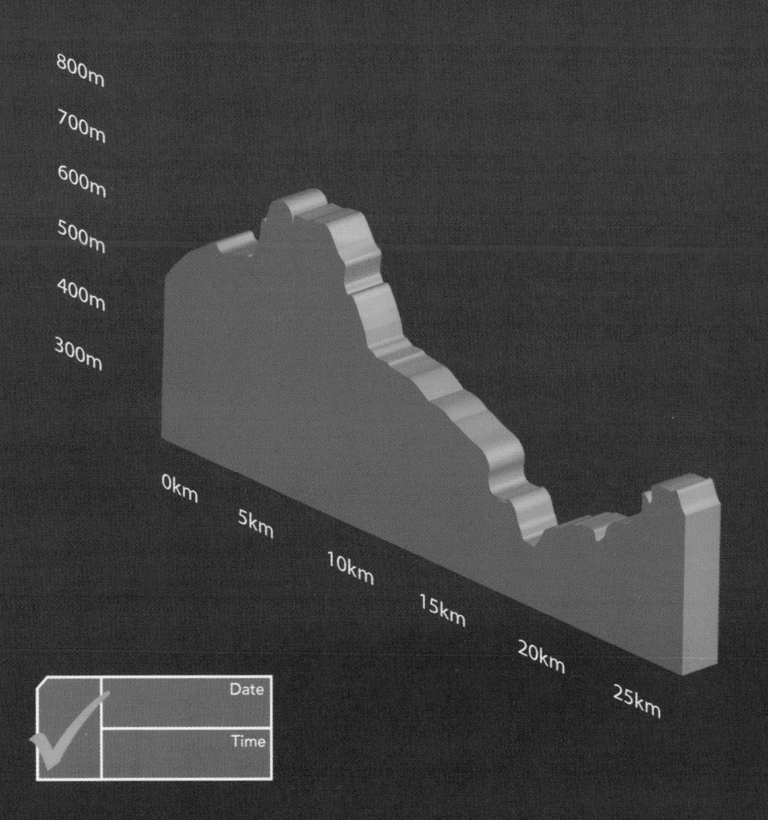

	Date
	Time

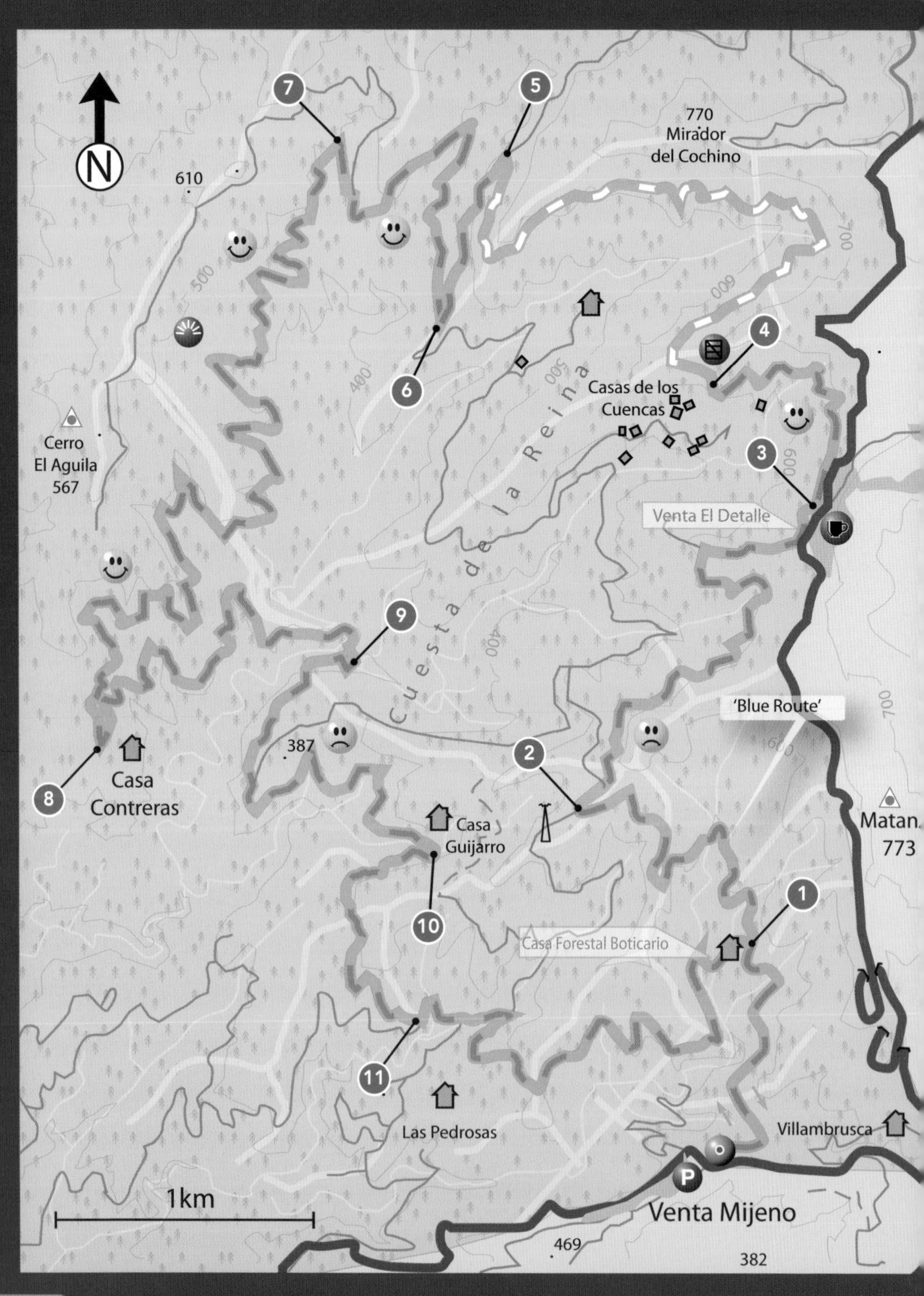

N
7
5
770
Mirador
del Cochino
610
500
700
600
4
6
400
500
Cuesta de la Reina
Casas de los
Cuencas
3
Cerro
El Aguila
567
600
Venta El Detalle
9
400
'Blue Route'
700
387
2
600
8
Casa
Contreras
Casa
Guijarro
Matan.
773
1
10
Casa Forestal Boticario
11
Las Pedrosas
Villambrusca
P
1km
Venta Mijeno
469
382

Route description

Start

Forest entrance

Follow the arrow into the forest, initially downhill until you see the Casa Forestal de Boticario and it's vulture pens through the trees. Pass the vulture information board and the gated entrance to El Boticatrio and head on up on the same track.

1 El Boticario

Take the right fork (the unchained one) at the junction and ride uphill toward the antenna. This is part of the Blue Route marked every 500m with small blue-capped concrete posts.

2 Antenna junction

Approach the junction leading to the antenna, but before you get there notice a chained track cutting up to the right. Pass the chain on the left and pedal uphill on a narrower forest track. Continue more steeply to a T-junction.

3 Venta junction

Our route heads left at the junction, but for those in need of some refuelling, take the right track up the hill to the road and the roadside bar of Venta El Detalle.

4 Casa de los Cuencas

The forest opens out above Casa de Los Cuencas. Pass the big metal gate and immediately fork rightwards. At the top, re-enter the forest and down narrowing doubletrack to a chain at the end of the track.

5 Chained junction

Turn left onto the main track and descend. Look out for the blue marker No 8 on your right. The next turn-off is 200m after this.

6 Easily missed junction

Look out for a semi-hidden track doubling back as the track meets the firebreak. Turn off, passing another chain and descend. Take care, it's easy to ride on past the turning.

7 Fork

Head down and left at the next fork – it's all downhill from here! Keep to the main track, ignoring the few minor tracks coming in from each side. Enjoy the views and set your bike to freewheel mode!

8 Casa Contreras

Just as you begin to think you've taken a wrong turning and are lost in the woods, a small ruin overrun with trees appears on the right. Breath a sigh of relief and follow the main trail down and left.

9 River crossing

What rides down must ride up! Cross the river bed on gravel and start the climb back home. Ignore any trails coming in from the left.

10 Casa Guijarro

Ride past a recently built trough, passing a track heading up behind your right shoulder. Keep on ascending straight ahead.

11 Don Ventura junction

The next main junction is marked with small wooden posts. Follow the white arrows all the way back to the road junction at El Boticario.

Turn right at the road and retrace your steps back to the start.

Section 3

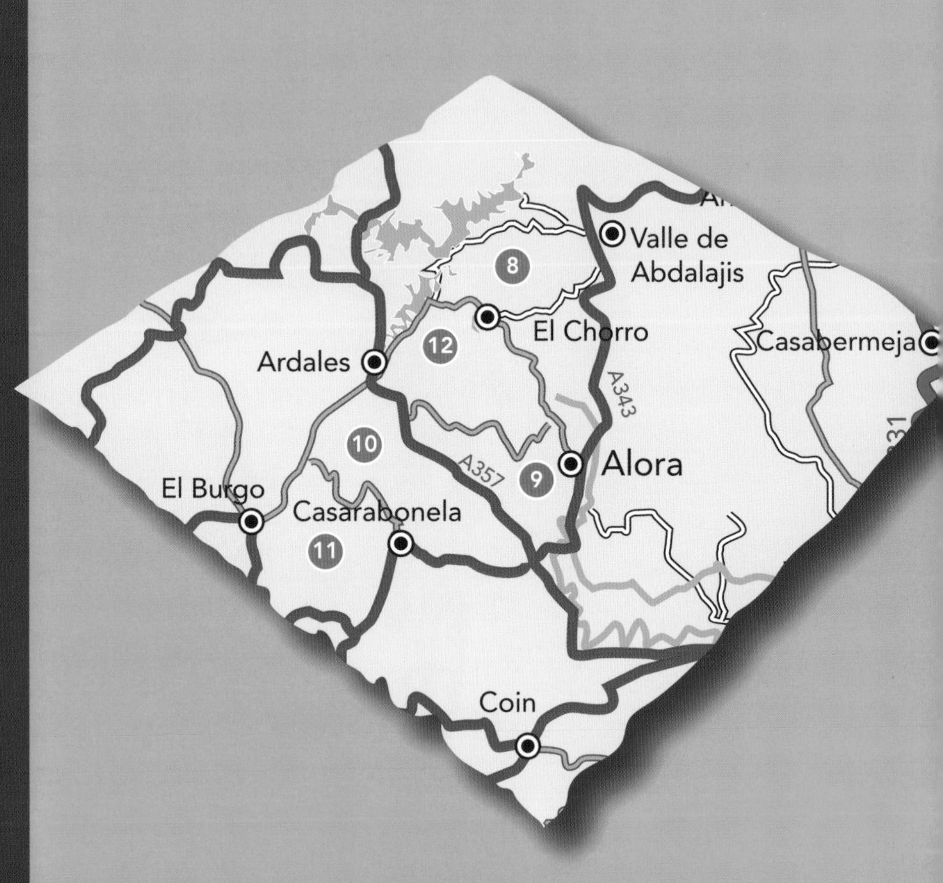

Tour de Huma	08	XC
Don Quixote	09	XC
Big Al, Little Al	10	XC
1000 Switchbacks	11	XC
El Moabo	12	XC / DH

Introduction

El Chorro is the Chamonix of southern Spain, with an international reputation for some of the finest climbing, walking and paragliding around. El Chorro and it's neighbouring mountains have some of the best mountain biking in Europe. Everyone who rides here inevitably comes back for more and the locals are pretty active in clearing new trails. From Moab-like slickrock to perfect forest singletrack it's all there if you look hard enough.

The huge open valley of the Rio Guadalhorce runs from the Ardales lakes, through the spectacular El Chorro Gorge which is surrounded by towering vertical cliffs, to the edge of the Sierra de las Nieves. The mountains are big and the opportunity for classic all-day XC adventures and shorter technical DH blasts are everywhere. The routes in this section are guaranteed to wear you out and make you grin in equal measures.

The routes in this section are in the main big XC circuits, but the greedy amongst you will notice that you can often cherry pick shorter singletrack rides armed with this guide and a handful of IGN maps. Ride the whole route, then go back for an evening blast another day!

You'll sometimes find in the coldest months that if the mountains are covered in cloud, a trip to the coast may be a better option, or if the coast is fog bound, the inland mountains will retain the best of the weather.

How to get there

The valley is well served by good road and rail links. The A357 runs inland from the coast and is shadowed by the main rail line north from Malaga. There are regular train services to Alora and the occasional train stopping at El Chorro itself. Recently improved roads lead into the mountains and the edges of the Sierra de las Nieves at Casarabonela, Alhaurin el Grande and Coin where the prophetic 'El Dorado' soap foresaw the influx of Brits quitting the UK for life in the sun.

Places to stay

Basing yourself at El Chorro gives you the widest number of accomodation options, from the climbers' campsite to bunkhouses and apartments at Finca la Campana and La Garganta, to self catering villas such as those at Finca Rocabella. El Chorro, though, is a little light on facilities – just a couple of small shops and bars so many people prefer to base themselves in and around the small town of Alora which offers decent supermarkets, shops, cafes, banks etc.

The only thing the area lacks is a decent bike shop, though simple spares can be obtained from Autos Estrada on Avenida de Cervantes. Major problems will take you to Coin (Autorecambios Cecilio, Avda Reina Sofia - on the main road into town opposite Aldi) or into Malaga.

SeasonallyUNadjusted.com who have been running biking holidays and guiding services in the area for years, know the trails better than anyone and have a huge network of superb routes throughout El Chorro, Alora and the Guadalhorce valley. Get in touch with them to ride the locals' best trails.

Summary

A big day out in all respects. Combining a huge XC loop, two enormous climbs and a perfect singletrack descent, this is a classic ride that everyone should do at least once. Looping around the huge limestone mountain of La Huma and passing under the vast cliffs of El Chorro, cameras are as essential as spare tubes on this route!

Once you leave 'El Kiosko' you are out in the wilderness until you descend into El Chorro village. Take plenty of food to get you up the hills as there's nowhere to refuel until you get back.

For a short blast you could also head into the forest from the railway station at El Chorro, toil up the fire road all the way to the top of the trees (WP 10) and once at the top turn right and blast all the way back down to the village.

El Kiosko Guadalhorce 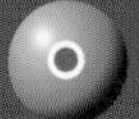

Classic 

Hard 

30 km 

700 m 

3 - 5 hrs 

Ardales 1:50,000 

Getting there

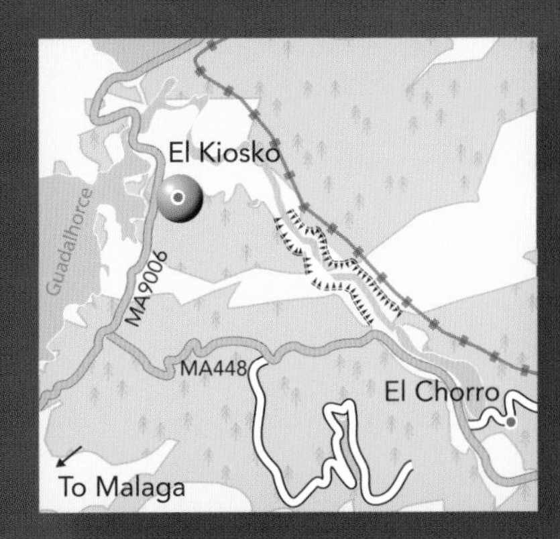

From the Costa del Sol head towards Malaga and take the A-357 inland to Ardales. Leave the main road at Ardales, following signs for El Chorro. Keep on this road, ignoring a turning to your right after about 5km. Carry on under a tunnel and park at the El Kiosko restaurant overlooking the lake.

Or

From the village of El Chorro, head north up the winding road past the gorge. Turn right at the T junction at the top, pass under the tunnel and park at El Kiosko restaurant.

Start point

Finish your coffee at El Kiosko, turn right and head northwards along the road, keeping the reservoirs on your left.

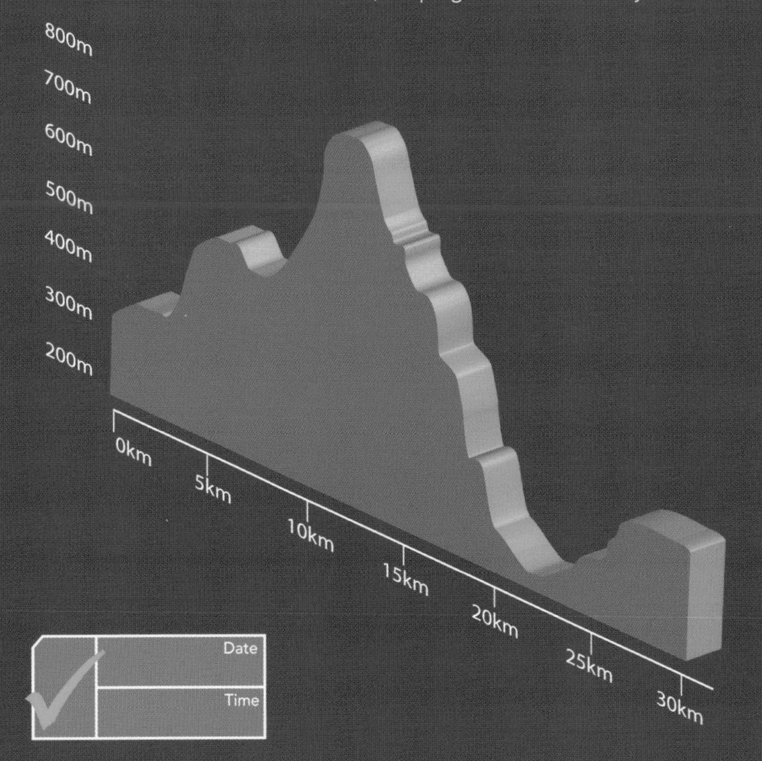

Date

Time

N
Embase del Conde de Guadalhorce
Valley de Abdalajis
Sierra Llana
611
837
102
600
500
300
El Kiosko
Pico del Convent
619
600
450
La Garganta
El Chorro Gorge
MA-464
372
El Chorro
Embalse Superior Tajo de la Encantada
441
Ardales
Alora
1km
1
2
3
13
14

Route description

1 El Kiosko

Start along the road, crossing two dams. Continue along the road, ignoring a road junction on the left and another on the right.

2 Road junction

At the next road junction, take the left fork signposted Valle de Abdalajis. Carry on along this road, passing a disused quarry until the road opens out and you can see a dirt track heading up on your right.

3 Road / Track junction

Leave the road here and get ready for the first of two big climbs. Stay to the main track all the way, keeping the enormous cliffs on your right. Stop for a well earned breather at a col, marked by a signpost pointing to a paragliding take-off area up and to the right of the track. Blast on down the other side until the first junction.

4 Track junction

Turn right at the bottom. Bear right at the next junction and continue to a crossroads.

5 Crossroads

Right again at the crossroads and wheeze your way up the enormous hill until you see a pair of gateposts straight ahead.

6 Gates

Take a left turn just before the gates (there's a signpost marking the MTB route here). Carry on up, stopping to take in the view at the highpoint before descending past the smelly goat farm and across the main col until you see a small wooden marker post at a junction. This is easy to miss – if you reach a ruin with a big waterbutt you have gone too far!

7 Wooden post

Take the right fork leaving the main track and follow the bumpy doubletrack down all the way. Ignore the uphill turnings.

8 Big cliff junction

Up and to your right is a big cliff. Bear right at the next turning and head westwards down a loose track, passing a small white goat farm. Stop at the gate on the right with a GR7 signpost about 300m after the farm.

9 GR7 gate

Go through the gate and head upwards for 500m until you get to a left turn with a red and white striped marker post. Head left and downhill to the edge of the forest.

10 Top of the trees

Turn left at the top of the trees, blast along the track taking the first easy right, and right again at next fork until the track ends at the start of the singletrack.

A non technical option here is to carry straight on down the fire road, missing out all of the singletrack, and taking you direct to El Chorro village.

Follow the obvious trail in front of you, down a steep 'bombhole' before riding up along increasingly exposed singletrack toward a ridge with a ruin.

11 Ruin & photo stop

Ride round to the right of the ruin, stop to catch your breath and take in the view before continuing westwards along the ridge. Cross an old threshing circle with another ruin on the left of the track. Shimmy your way down some of the most perfect snaking singletrack you'll ever ride until you reach the fireroad.

12 Fireroad

Turn right and ride uphill for about 1km until you see a yellow sign marking the entrance to a track off to the left with a chain across it.

Take the chained track, passing a beehive village and descend tricky switchbacks on singletrack all the way to the bottom.

13 El Chorro village

Turn left and head back to El Chorro village.

14 Back to the start

Leave the village on the road heading across the dam and turning right toward the gorge at the junction. Continue uphill on the road for 5km, turn right at the T junction and spin back to El Kiosko for a well earned swim in the lakes.

bikefax

09 Guadalhorce & El Chorro Don Quixote

Summary

Miguel de Cervantes, the Spanish Shakespeare and author of Don Quixote, spent a few years as a tax collector in nearby Alora. Much like the novel, following this trail takes you on a journey past windmills, ancient ruins, olive groves and goat-ridden sierras. Add Sancho Panza with his Mule (or was it a Camelbak?) and all's set for a classic Spanish adventure.

Whilst most of the route isn't technically difficult, this is a long route with a 'traditional' feel. Enjoy the views on the way up, watch out for impromptu 'gates' strung across the trail with nothing more than a rag to warn you, especially between the red and white mast and the goat farm! For a more technical descent at Bobastro have a look at Route 11 - the La Mesa Descent.

Stop en route for a bite to eat in El Chorro and enjoy the spin back through lemon, orange and olive groves.

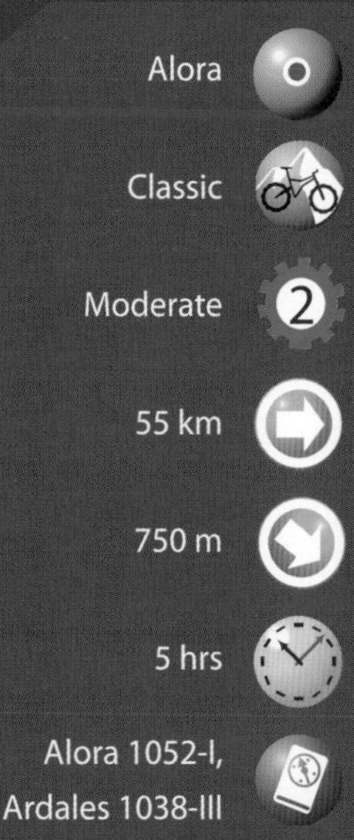

Getting there

From the coast

Head inland along the A357. Take the exit for Alora and continue following the signs for Alora. Keeping the town and castle on the hill to your left, cross the river until you reach the Los Caballos restaurant. Turn left, then left again at the roundabout and skirt round Alora until you reach the traffic lights. Go straight across and continue towards Cararatraca.

From El Chorro & the north

Head south toward Alora and at the edge of town go right. Carry on along the road signposted to Carratraca, until a restaurant called 'Conejitos' appears on your right. Follow the road along a right hand bend. After almost 3km you will see a pine forest descending to the road.

If you are approaching Alora from the North on the A357, you may wish to park at 'Conejitos' and start and finish your ride here.

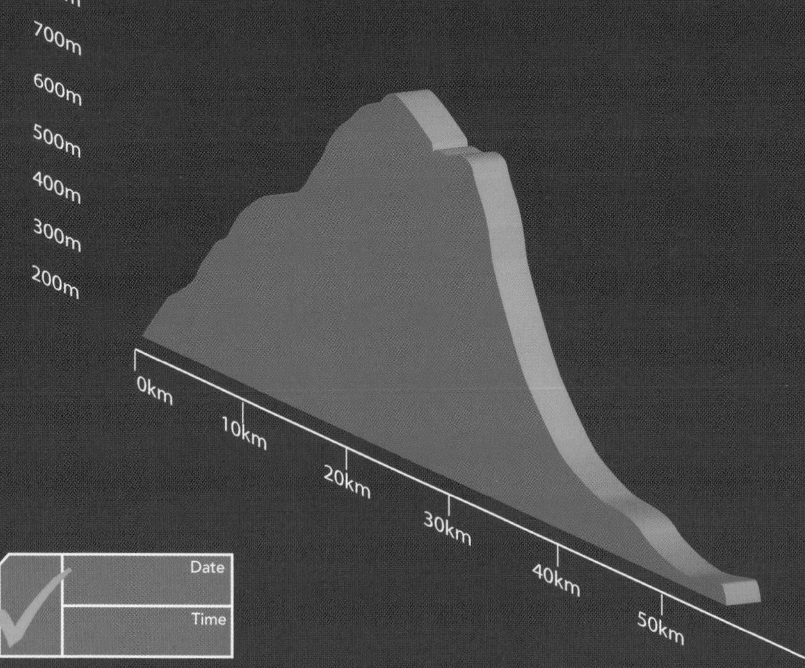

	Date
✓	Time

Route description

Start

At the start of the pine forest a sign denotes 'rockfall for 9km', just after this a white house set above the road on the right, park at the dirt track junction and start the route here.

1 White house

Follow the dirt track up behind the white house and continue winding your way uphill.

2 Junction

Ignore the junction off to the right and carry on up with ever expanding views over the Guadalhorce Valley, El Chorro and beyond. Ignore side tracks heading downhill – the only way is up (baby...).

3 Fork

Just after the first downward section since you started, the track forks. Point your handlebars left and traverse round the south side of the mountain under the wind turbines.

4 Wind turbines

Stop for a quick 'tilt' under the windmills then head downhill to the south west on a fast, twisting dirt track.

5 Turning point

Easily missed turning. After a tight U turn, the track continues downhill. Spot the track off to your right and make sure you don't miss the turning. You'll find it just as the trees lining your right hand side fade out. Take the mud track, passing a red and white stripey mast and carry on for a couple of kilometres, riding straight on at a crossroads.

6 Lonely house

Pass an isolated house on your right. At the next junction pedal sharply upwards, continuing past another house. Watch yourself here as there is a hidden gate placed just round the sharp right hander as you head downhill.

7 Gates

Carry on through the goat farm. Care is needed here to spot the sporadic semi-invisible homemade wire gates across the trail. Look out for plastic bottles and rags tied to chainlink strung across the track. Relax after the second green gate and blast down ignoring minor tracks off to each side.

8 GR marker posts

Eventually you reach a junction with a track coming in from below and to your left, marked with a red and white striped wooden marker post.

Carry straight on down the hill around some steep corners until you reach a sudden rude climb up to a small pass cut into the hill above a smelly goat farm (down to your left). Rollercoaster your way down and up on more amenable gradients until you reach the tarmac of the road to Bobastro.

9 Bobastro

Once you reach the tarmac and spectacular view, turn right and begin the tarmac climb, passing the Moorish Church sign to your left. Continue steeply uphill. Turn right at the T junction and spin past El Chorro gorge.

DO NOT STOP HERE FOR PHOTOS – THE CRASH BARRIERS TELL THEIR OWN TALE. Instead carry on to the El Pilar Restaurant and get your photos there.

10 El Chorro

Turn left across the dam and head up through the village to the railway station (shops and places to eat here as well as a Fuente on the switchback by the phonebox and climbing shop). Leave El Chorro behind passing the La Garganta restaurant, and climb a little way uphill until you can take a right fork signposted 'Finca la Campana'.

11 Road junction

Carry on past several houses and continue past the sign to Finca la Campana. After a couple of kms you reach a three way junction.

12 Junction

Take the middle fork upwards under the pylons and scream down the other side, crossing under the railway a little after a ford. All the time you are making for the obvious blue bridge.

13 Blue bridge

Drop down under the bridge (take care for traffic as you exit the hidden junction). Cross over the low bridge and pick up the tarmac. Carry on through the village of Las Mellizas and out the other side.

14 Road to Alora

Turn left at the T junction and pedal back to the traffic lights in Alora. Stop for a well deserved snack and return to the start. (It's at this point that stashing a car or riding from here at the start of the day suddenly makes a lot of sense!).

Convent
Alora
MA-224
Río Guadalhorce
13
14
397
282
Los Conejitos
A 357
Sierra de Aguas
768
808
2
3
576
939
1
4
668
5
824
8
6
7
1km
300
400
200
700
800
500
550

Summary

Take a tour of the Sierra de Alcaparain for a big climb, great views and a testing Andalucian switchback descent. Start by traversing round the mountain, before making a big climb up to the summit plateau of the Alcaparain at 1150m. From here tackle the fall line head on to plummet straight down to the other side.

The views across the Sierra de las Nieves on the way up, and towards El Chorro on the way down, make this trail a photographers heaven and the riding is just as spectacular.

It's certainly worth getting to grips with switchbacks on a route like the 'Tour de Huma', before you try this trail. as taking a tumble on the way down here will land you in a rocky, prickly mess in the gorse on the side of the trail – you'll be pulling out the prickles for weeks at the very least!

Ardales 

Expert 

Extreme 

17 km

610 m 

2 - 3 hrs 

Ardales 1038
Serrato 1037 

Getting there

Follow the A357 from Malaga toward Ardales. Just outside Ardales (a few kms after an isolated petrol station) the road heads over a pass; the Puerto de Malaga, carry on over the pass, and note the tree lined track on your left.

Take the turn off at the bottom of the hill for Ardales and then follow the signs back onto the A357 back toward Malaga. Just before the pass, about 500m short of the line of trees, there is a turn off onto a dirtrack at the end of a long section of barriers.

Head along the track running parallel to the main road, then follow the track uphill until you get to a three way junction next to a water deposit and with a Helipad to your right.

Start point

Park at the three way junction with a water deposit and Helipad to your right. Start here.

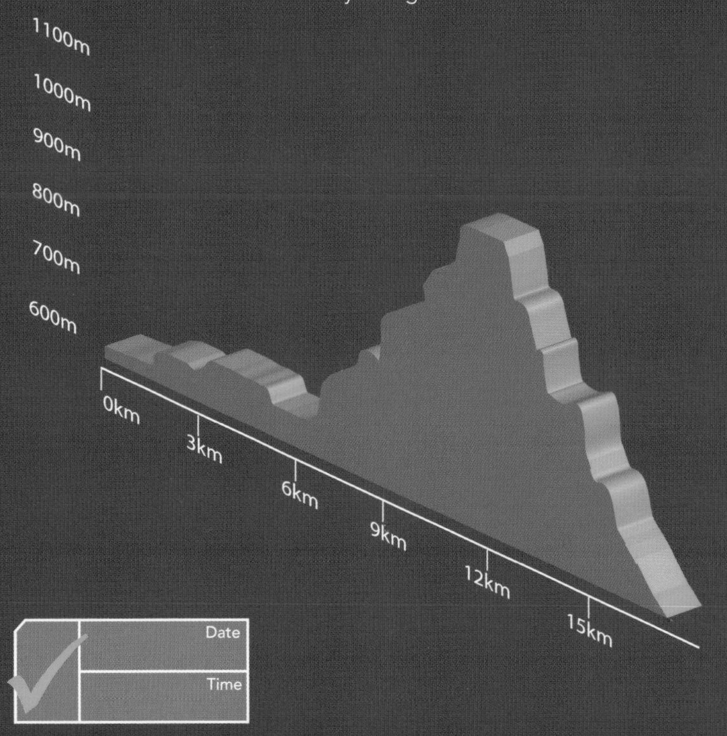

Date

Time

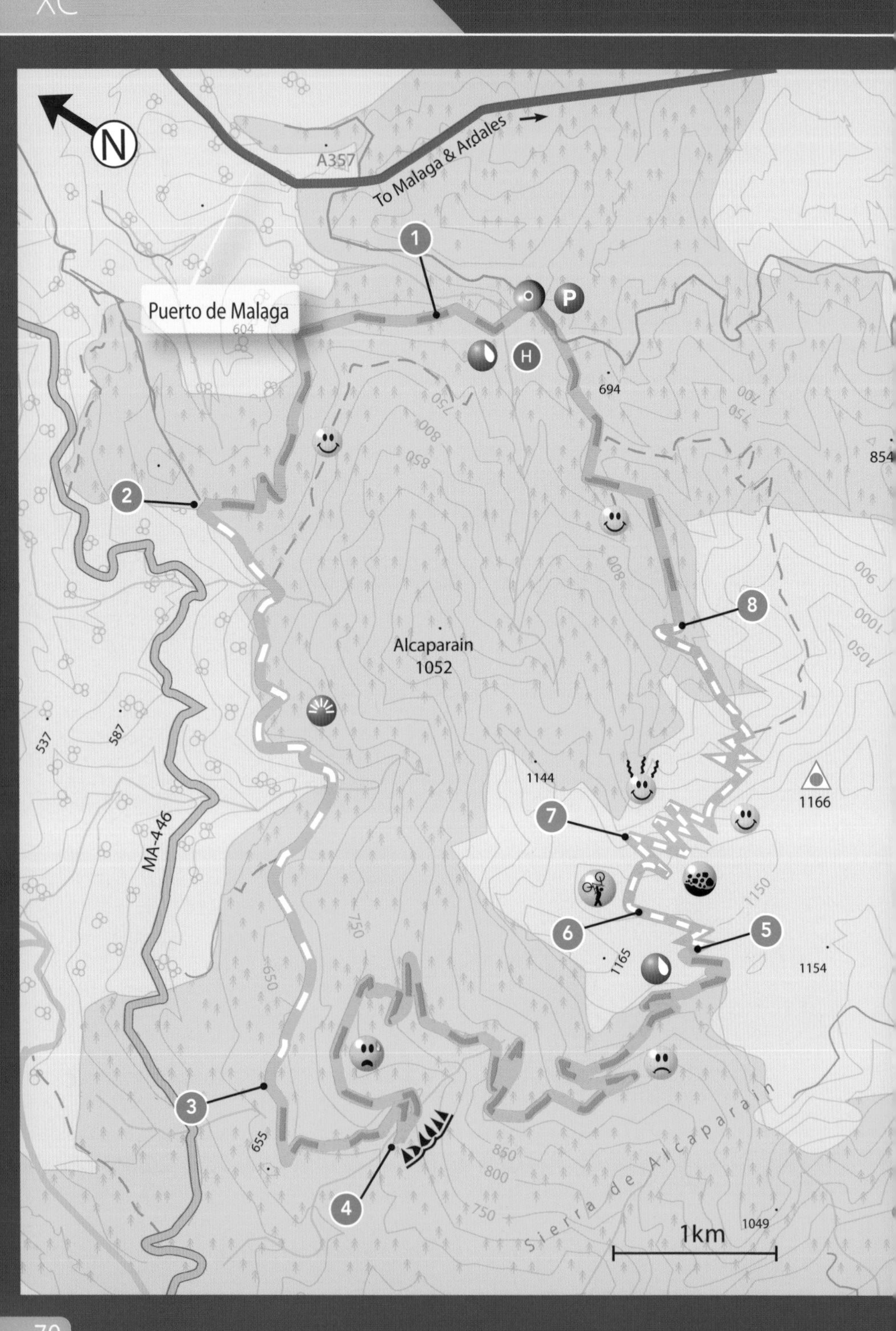
N
A357
To Malaga & Ardales →
1
Puerto de Malaga
604
P
H
694
700
750
750
800
850
854
2
800
900
1000
1050
8
Alcaparain
1052
537
587
1144
1166
MA-446
7
1150
750
6
5
1165
1154
650
655
850
800
750
3
4
Sierra de Alcaparain
1049
1km

Route Description

Start

Head along the right-hand of the three trails with the water deposit on your right.

1 Fork in track

Turn left at the first fork and rollercoaster your way around the hill until you reach a junction.

2 T-junction

At the junction turn left and continue round the back of the mountain. The views just get better and better.

3 Junction

As you reach another juntion take the next left and carry on around.

4 Start of big climb

After a few kilometres you ride underneath a big craggy area. The track splits here with ours doubling back and rising toward the crags, whilst the other way continues straight on. Keep on going along the main trail, ignoring the odd minor turning. As you get higher, the zig zags get closer until you pierce the last crags and pass a white water butt on the left.

5 Summit plateau

A hundred metres on past the water butt, you see a series of cairned paths off to the left. Ignore the first minor one and take the next larger one heading across the plateau on narrow singletrack.

6 Cairned junction

Halfway across the plateau (all but the gnarliest will have dabbed a few times by now!) you will come to a small cairn where the trail splits. Head rightwards and carry on until the next junction. It's difficult to ride all the way here and you may find yourself having to carry your bike over the next 100m or so!

7 'The Way Down'

As the amphitheatre below begins to come into view, the path reaches a T junction. Turn right and follow the increasingly good singletrack rightwards. Once you pass the first 'cobbled' section, you know you're on the right line.

The switchbacks start tight and carry on downwards with longer and longer straights between each one. Nowhere is the trail easy, and it doesn't let up until the bottom!!!

8 Fireroad

Back at a fire road, sadly the singletrack ends and the trail continues along the fire road. Follow the track down, ignoring a track heading up to your right, and back to the start point.

Summary

The Sierra Prieta is a stunning peak standing high above the Guadalhorce valley, and this huge loop takes in the whole of the eastern side of the mountain to form a great epic day out. The first half of the trail is visible from many kilometres away and just asks to be ridden!

There are several tricky singletrack variants or an easier tarmac and dirt track version of this exhilating ride into the beautiful white village of Casarabonela. If you can take you eyes off the track for a moment you are often rewarded with glimpses of Golden and Bonelli's Eagles, falcons and mountain goats.

Straightforward or technical, the choice is yours. Either way you'll have some tough climbs and fast descents. The singletrack is pure spanish adrenaline; switchback after switchback with plenty of loose rocks liberally scattered to keep you on your toes at all times.

Alozaina 

Expert 

Hard 

27 km 

850 m 

3-5 hrs 

See note 

Getting there

From Marbella and the Costa:

Take the Ojen road which heads inland from the N340 at the La Cañada Shopping Centre. Take the exit into Coin and at the roundabout on the edge of town, bear left following signs for Tolox and Alozaina. Keep going until you reach a roundabout at Alozaina.

From Malaga:

Follow the A357 inland for about 30km. Take the exit marked 'Casarabonela and Zalea' and follow the road until a junction with Casarabonela ahead and Alozaina to the left. Follow the road leftwards until the roundabout at Alozaina.

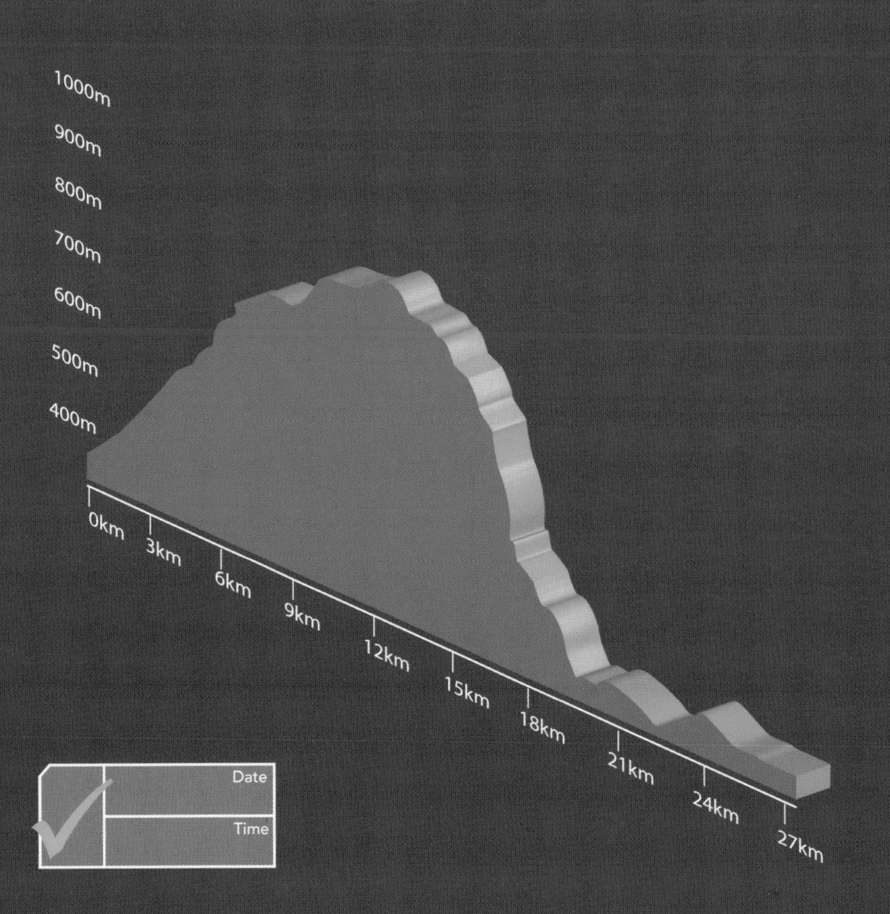

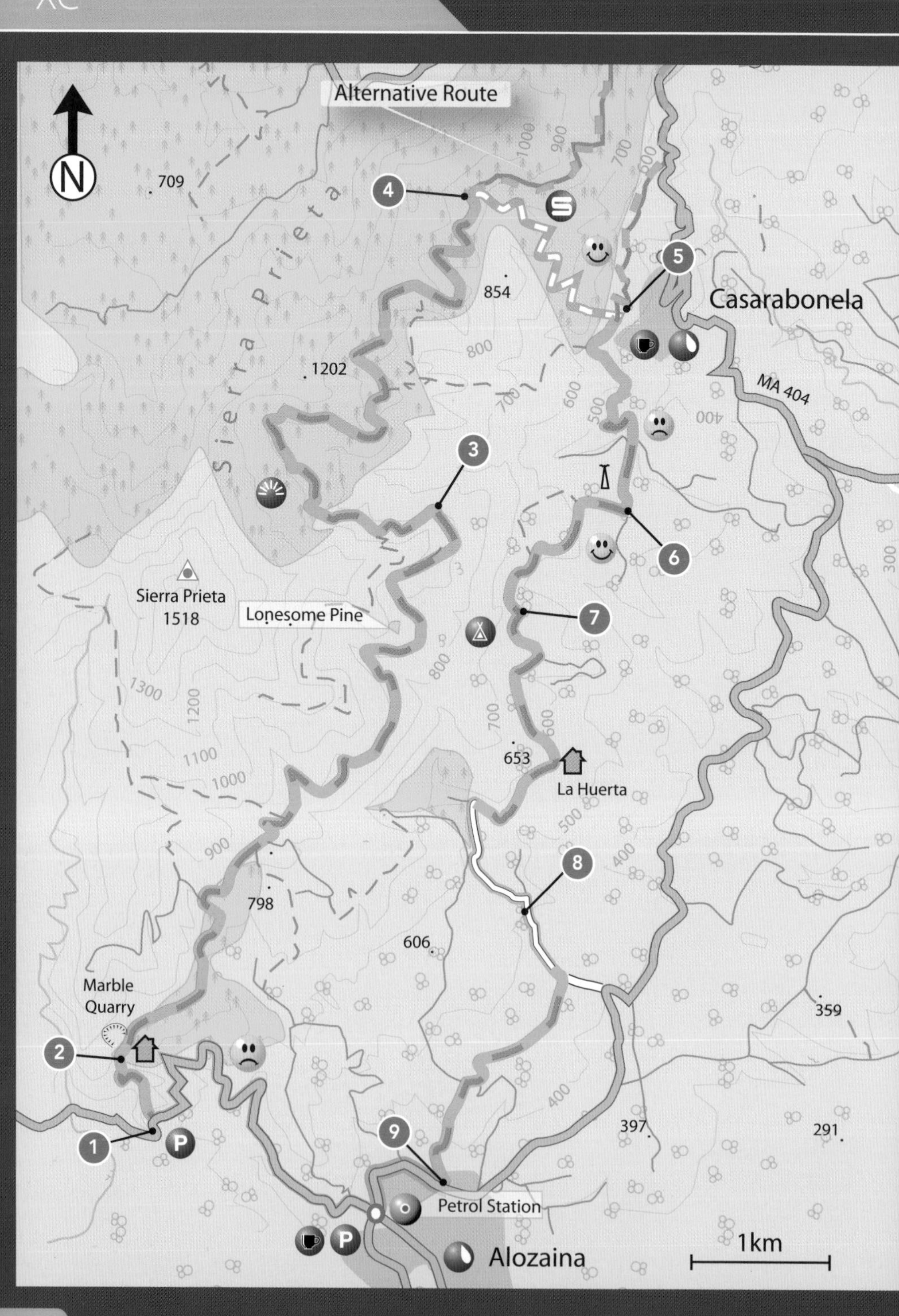
Alternative Route
N
709
Sierra Prieta
4
854
1202
Casarabonela
MA 404
3
5
6
7
Sierra Prieta
1518
Lonesome Pine
653
La Huerta
8
798
606
Marble
Quarry
2
1
9
Petrol Station
Alozaina
397
291
359
1km

Route description

Start

Park near the roundabout in Alozaina. There are several cafes for pre and post ride refuelling here (Venta Jaca amongst others is recommended) and water can be found a little way into Alozaina at a fuente on the right just before the stone archway. There are shops for trail snacks just beyond.

There is no water until Casarabonela and you'll be in the sun all day so fill up your Camelbak early.

1 Junction

Head uphill on the road, signposted 'Yunquera', for about 6 km until you can take a turning on the right onto a dirt track marked with an old wooden 'Junta de Andalucia' sign.

Those with more than one vehicle can miss this road climb out by leaving a car in Alozaina and another by the quarry buildings.

2 Marble quarry

Passing the incredible marble slabs on your left, the route continues along the dirt track. Ignore any minor turnings on both sides. Eventually turn a corner into a huge amphitheatre with a 'lonesome pine' on the ridge above as you approach.

3 Ampitheatre traverse

Carry on along the same track contouring round the bowl and trending downwards as you go, to reach a point where the track takes a sharp left hander under a cliff. Continue from here until you reach a wooded ridge with a trail running down it's spine.

4 Start of switchbacks

Descend down the ridge on rocky singletrack taking care to follow all the switchbacks and not be tempted by the hikers shortcuts. After the endless, but easy angled, zigzag descent, stop at a big fallen tree.

Take the right hand trail and carry on down on far steeper switchbacks to the edge of the village. Follow your nose from here to find the centre of Casarabonela where there is a square, fuente and several good places to eat.

Bar Nuevo down to your left in the square by the viewpoint is recommended, as is the ice cream shop just below the parking. You can fill up your water bottles in the square just under the church.

5 Leaving Casarabonbela

Easier said than done. Head to the south past the ice cream shop (Heladeria) along Calle Alta, keeping your height as you ride through the narrow streets which eventually open up as you head downhill. Carry on back up the other side, keeping right at any forks.

There are a series of red 'campamiento' signs painted on walls, rocks etc to follow and a tiled sign. Follow the 'Camino de Alozaina'– MA 403.

6 Antenna Corner

Turn right at the junction at the top of the hill by the mast. Look out for the large white information sign. Carry on climbing along the Camino del Naranjal and just keep going until you reach the Sierra Prieta Campamiento at the top of a stiff concrete climb.

7 Fast descent

The next stretch is a long fast descent to a junction. Catch your breath at the top of the climb and then carry straight on downhill on a rough dirt track. Continue trending downhill passing the odd house and ignoring turn offs. Eventually you will make a left turn where the track opens out and you head down a long straight with a new looking house at the bottom.

Take care to watch out for the yappy dogs and bear right at the bottom. Enjoy the track through the olives with some great little jumps until you get to a junction.

8 Track junction

Make a right turn uphill at the junction, pedal up and over and continue along the track ; the Camino de Callejon. Go straight across at the cobbled descent (best taken straight down the middle) and continue along the walled track to the main road.

9 Main road

Turn right and crank your way along the road uphill toward Alozaina and a well earned beer.

Singletrack variants

There are a number of singletrack descents marked on the map. All are very technical with switchbacks, reasonable drop offs and plenty of rocks. It's easy to lose the rideable trail on a couple of them. Each is Grade 4.

The easy option

For those wanting to give the technical riding a miss, you can easily turn this into a longer laid back ride around the flanks of Sierra Prieta. To do this follow the route as far as WP 4 and the start of the technical descent. Continue straight on along the track as far as a minor road. At the minor road turn right and follow it into Casarabonela. From here pick up the trail again at WP5 and continue to the end.

Note on maps

To cover the route thoroughly you will need:

Alora 1052-I

El Burgo 1051-I

Yunquera 1051-III

Villa Franco de Guadalhorce 1052-II (very briefly)

Summary

This route is a personal favourite. It includes some truly awesome riding, and what gives the ride it's real character are the solid rock slabs that make for exceedingly fun obstacles. The first section of trail snakes its way down fast and elegant singletrack taking you over slabs, and whalebacks and in places it's more than a little reminiscent of the famous slickrock of Moab, hence the name.

The second descent of the route is different again; the solid rock trail cut out of the hillside is a total white knuckle ride. When you get to the bottom, look back up and you'll wonder just how the hell you got down it.

Don't be put off in the slightest by the on-road slogs because the singletrack is some of the best around but if you're riding a DH rig, you might try and get some kindly soul to take you up the road climbs.

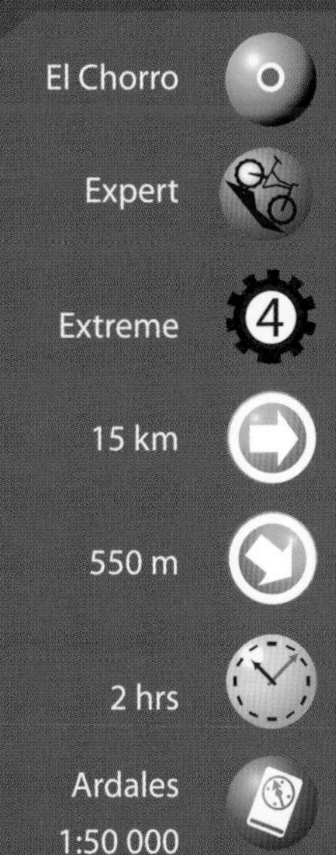

Getting there

El Chorro is situated about 35 km north west of Malaga. To get to El Chorro from the coast, take the A357 from Malaga to Ardales. At Ardales turn right on to the MA444. After 6 km turn right again for El Chorro.

Start point

Start in the village of El Chorro.

The best way to do this route is to get some friendly soul to drive you all the way to the lake at the top, have a couple of coffees at El Kiosko and blast on down. If they were going to be really super nice to you, they would meet you at the bottom of the Kiosko singletrack, and give you a lift up the road to the top of the Kiosko track. Failing this, you'll have to get your legs working and accept the road climbs as a necessary evil.

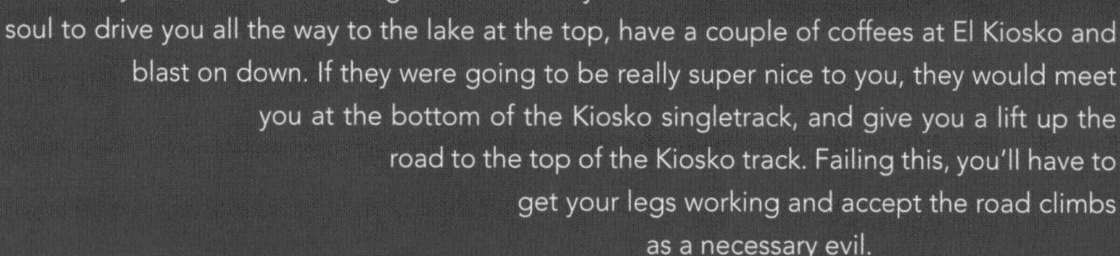

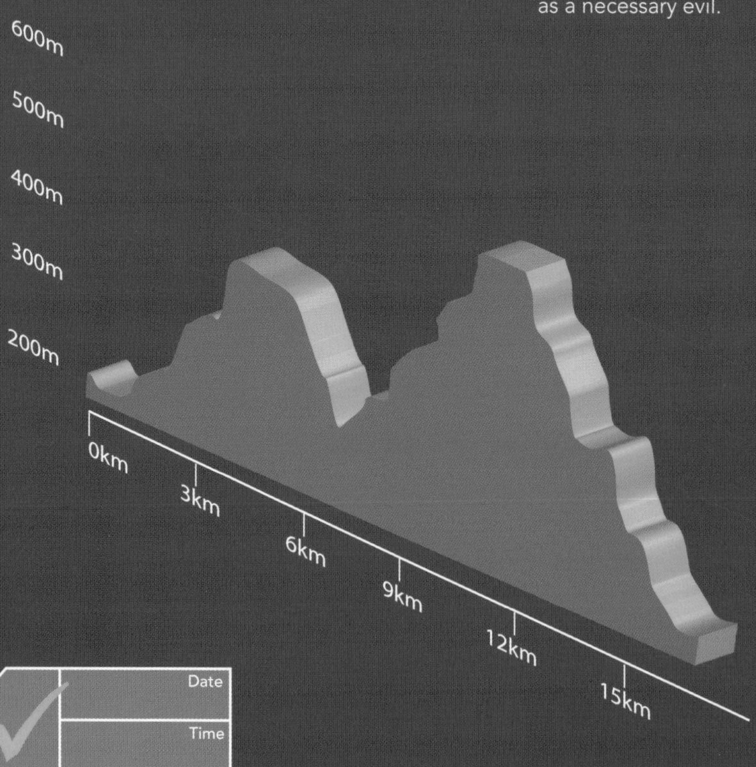

Route description

Start

Park in El Chorro, then head down the road and out of the village to the dam. Cross the dam wall and turn right towards Ardales.

The first road section takes you past the entrance to the very impressive El Chorro gorge and you can just make out the narrow walkway and bridge built in1921 for the king of Spain to view his recently completed reservoir complex.

If you've not managed to find a friendly driver, just spin your way up, passing a left turn to Bobastro. Go as far as a T-junction at the top. Now and again you might just glimpse the superb singletrack in the gully below you.

Turn right at the junction and ride along watching out for a piece of singletrack disappearing steeply up to your right opposite a gravel lay-by and a lane to a campsite.

At this point, if you've ridden up you'll probably want to head straight for the singletrack, but carry on another kilometre and buy yourself a coffee and some lunch at El Kiosko bar and café. This'll set up nicely for the descent.

1 El Kiosko

From El Kiosko, pedal back down the road, through the tunnel and go as far as the track to the campsite at Parque Ardales (on the right). Opposite this is a metal barrier and a sign warning against starting fires. Behind this a faint line of singletrack heading steeply upwards.

2 Turn off to campsite

Go up the singletrack, don't be put off by the initial steepness because this only lasts for short distance. After riding over a rock slab you will find yourself traversing along the right hand side of the hill for a few metres before the trail dives off over to the left. Take a breather here sucking in the views and give yourself time to prepare for what is possibly some of the best singletrack you've ever ridden.

The trail begins with fast and narrow singletrack which snakes you in and out of the trees. This soon spits you out into the open and onto your first series of rock slabs.

Watch out for the off camber slabs, although great fun they are tricky to ride. The trail reaches the road all too soon.

3 Metal barrier

Make your way around the metal barrier and onto the road itself. You may recognise this from the journey up. Head left back down the hill watching out for a trail off to the right on a small rise after roughly 50m. Just over the brow of the hill you'll spot a line off to the left and down the biggest rock slab yet.

Just as you think it can't get any better you reach the most fun slab yet, the 'Roller-coaster'. Continuing down the trail over yet more 'laugh out loud' type obstacles it begins to level off bringing you to a dry river bed. Follow this for a few metres before joining the trail again on the left and back to the road.

4 Road junction to Bobastro

On the road turn right. You are now on the road to Bobastro which you passed on the way up. If you look up to the left you can just make out the junction.

Prepare yourself for another road slog. Watching the road as it winds its way upwards

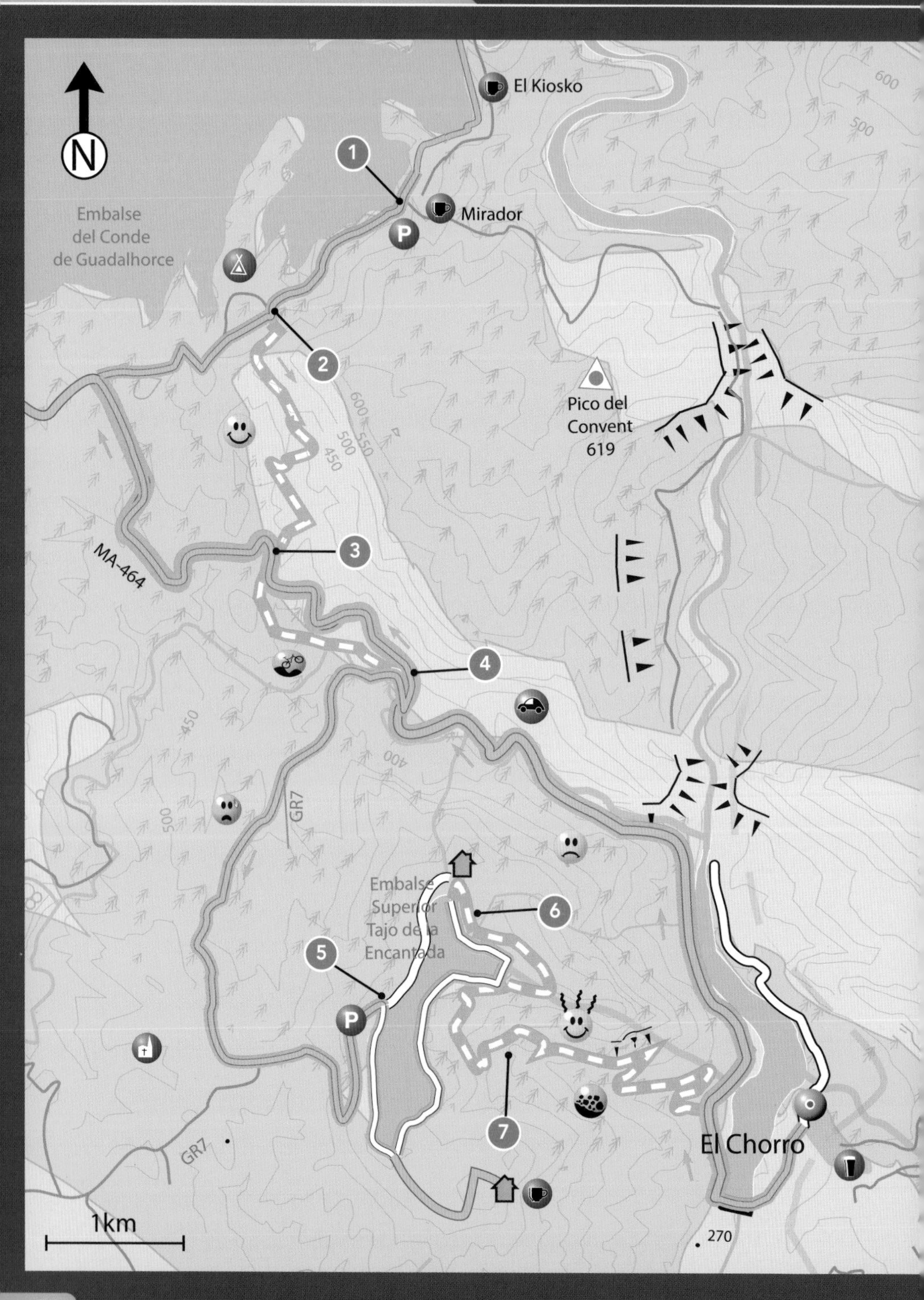
N
El Kiosko
Mirador
Embalse
del Conde
de Guadalhorce
Pico del
Convent
619
MA-464
GR7
Embalse
Superior
Tajo de la
Encantada
El Chorro
270
1km
600
500
550
450
400
1
2
3
4
5
6
7

can be depressing but fear not, the climb is a lot easier than it looks. Ignore any dirt-tracks off to the sides and follow the tarmac up and round a series of hairpins. Before long you will come up along side the reservoir at the top of La Mesa.

5 Reservoir

Hop over the barrier to your left and onto the concrete path along the side of the reservoir. Follow this anti-clockwise around, and you'll find yourself riding along the dam wall itself. If you haven't got a head for heights it may not be wise to peer over to the right. If you do, about halfway along you'll notice a piece of singletrack heading off a track into the trees.

Make note of this because this is where you'll be heading. At the end of the dam take the track off to the right heading back on yourself and underneath the dam itself.

This track drops quite suddenly, but be sure to watch out for the trail off to your left (red and white marker post) immediately after the track levels out. This is the singletrack you may have spotted from the top of the dam.

6 Red & white marker post

Again it may be worth taking a breather here before dropping back down. Following the trail it starts off fast and flowy through the trees taking you round a series of sharp bends. Do not be fooled though, it soon gets steeper and more technical as you round a switch back and traverse around to the other side of the valley.

7 Rocky switchbacks

Here the trail is a mixture of solid rock and loose gravel, with a choice of lines between ruts to choose from. As the trail progresses, you'll find yourself swinging round a couple of switch backs where the trail changes character and sends you straight downwards over loose terrain and under the impossible looking cliffs.

Towards the bottom you reach a wider gravel track. Follow this to the right and back down to the road and the El Chorro reservoir. At the bottom follow your tyre tracks back towards El Chorro and to the car, stopping to look at back at the seemingly impossible line, for a well deserved coffee at the station café.

Section 4

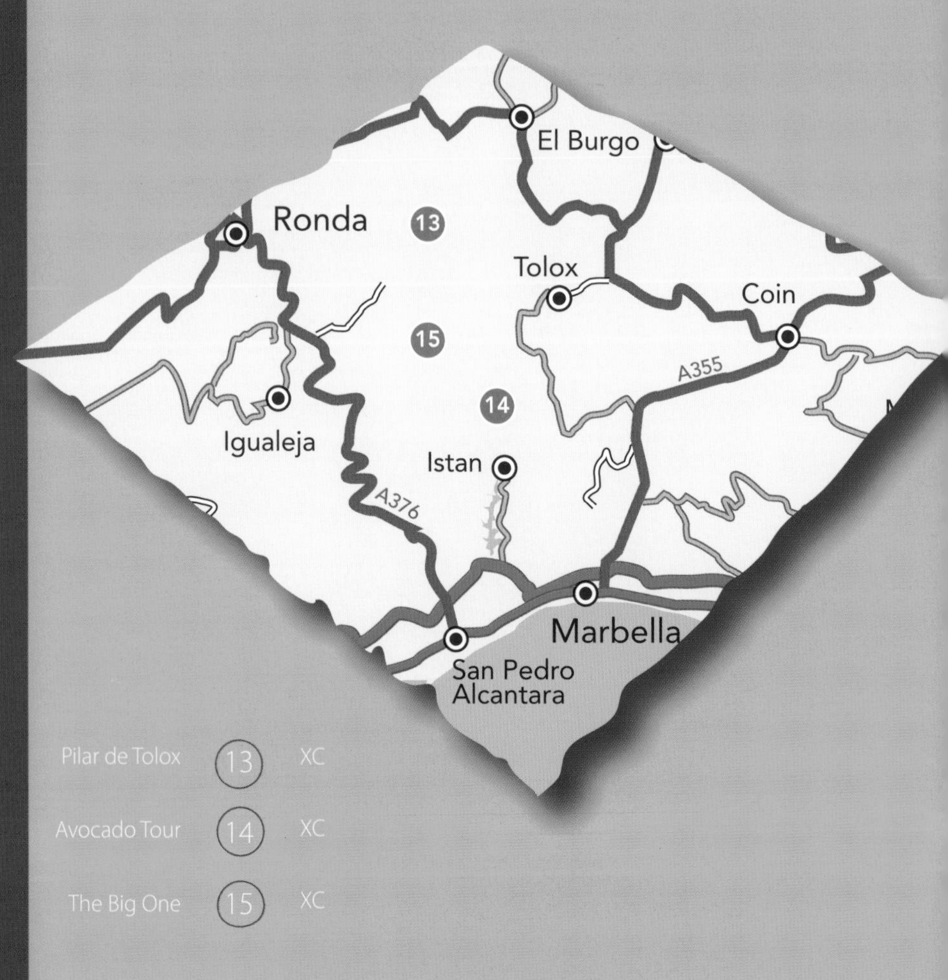

Introduction

Sitting on the beach on the western Costa del Sol or mooching around the super-yachts in Puerto Banus, it's easy to forget that a true mountain wilderness is towering behind you. Known collectively as the Sierra de las Nieves – the Mountains of the Snows – this group of mountains boasts some unique flora, an endless network of dirt tracks to explore and quiet, 'off the beaten track' riding.

For those with a thirst for adventure there's stacks to go at here.This is the area above all others, is ripe for weeks and weeks of exploring. As a UNESCO Biosphere reserve and Natural Park, the area is well served by park wardens protecting amongst other things the unique 'Pinsapo' pines which occur in the high Sierras, here and nowhere else in the world. Access is particularly tightly controlled when there is a high fire risk and whole areas can be closed to the public in the summer.

Getting there

Most people will access the Sierra de las Nieves from the coast. The main road north from San Pedro de Alcantara near Marbella, the A376, takes you into to the heart of the mountains on it's way to Ronda, and is worth the drive in itself.

If you are based in the Guadalhorce Valley you have a choice. Take the picturesque back roads from Ardales or Casarabonela and meander your way slowly across to Ronda, before heading south on the A376, or blast down the main roads to the Costa and then head back uphill on the Ronda road.

Food & drink

Ronda is a great place to explore and has all the amenities you'd expect from a large town. The Marbella/Ronda road has few places to stop for food, until you get to the Las Quejigales turning, and the isolated Bar la Raja and Pension El Navasillo. Once in the park there is no food or drink for miles. Often even the springs run dry so make sure you are self sufficient on the hill.

Istan has a delightful Andalucian 'White Village' feel despite being so close to Marbella. An hour in one of the many tapas bars here is time well spent!

Accomodation

Accomodation is easy to find on the coast and around Ronda. There are numerous campsites on the N340 coast road and a couple within a short drive of Ronda, such as Camping el Sur on the Ronda-Algeciras road or El Abogao on the Ronda/Campillos road, heading eastwards.

Bike shops & services

Bike Station, Marbella. C. Nuestra Señora de Gracia 28. www.bikemarbella.com

Radikal Bike, Estepona – Calle Ceuta, Estepona (29680) (behind the bus station) phone 952 80 14 07

There are also several bike shops in Ronda

There is a hospital with A&E department on the Eastern side of Ronda on the ringroad.

Contacts & more info

The guys in the local bike shops will point out the main dirt track routes, and a quick Google for biking round here will throw up loads of ideas in the same vein. A couple of good sources local info are:

www.mtbmalaga.com
www.bikerones.com
www.ronda.net/101km for the enduro

There is also a great guidebook to the whole area. 'Sierra de las Nieves Guia del Excursionista' published by Editorial La Serrania suggests easy bike routes and details all the walking trails. which can sometimes turn up gems in addition to the routes described in this guide.

Summary

Arguably the most 'All mountain' route in the western half of this guide. It's high, remote and technically tricky, and you'll need to be well equipped with food, water, clothes and bike bits, competent in navigation and be blessed with good weather as you are miles from anywhere, should anything go wrong. This route can be snowbound from November to April – check before you leave and don't attempt the route if bad weather is forecast at any time of the year, as there's no escape from thunderstorms once you are commited to the high mountain plateau.

After an initial five kilometre climb on a perfectly angled track, you head off into the wilderness and singletrack your way to the base of the Torrecilla, the highest mountain in Malaga Province at 1918m. After a quick detour on foot to the summit (you've come this far after all!) retrace your steps

Las Quejigales 

Epic 

 Hard 

 17 km 

 840 m 

4 hrs 

Sierra de las Nieves 

to the Puerto de los Pilones and drop into the feisty Cañada del Cuerno descent more reminiscent of the Canadian Rockies than the Costa del Sol.

This area contains some of the largest stands of the uber-rare Pinsapo Pine which only grows in the high Sierra de las Nieves, and is the main reason for the area to be a UNESCO Biosphere Reserve. It goes without saying that fire is the biggest hazard to this Natural Park. Careful with those cigars!

Getting there

From the coast leave the N340 at San Pedro and take the Ronda road (A-473) heading inland. A little after the KM 14 marker you see a huge 'Sierra de las Nieves' sign and a signposted turning on your right for Conejeras and Las Quejigales. Leave the main road here and drive carefully, following the signs to Las Quejigales 10km up the dirt track which is bumpy in places.

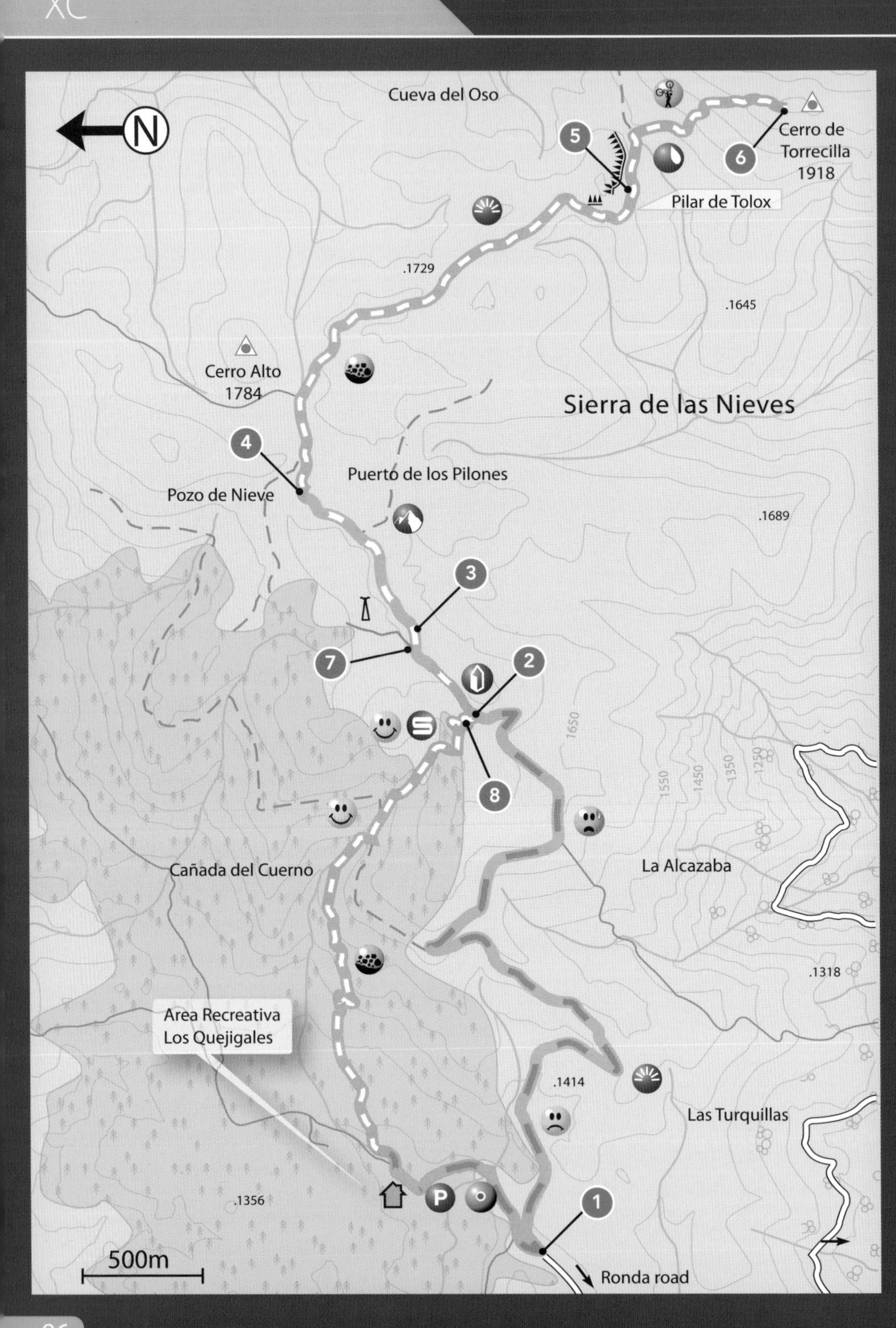
N
Cueva del Oso
5
6
Cerro de Torrecilla 1918
Pilar de Tolox
.1729
.1645
Cerro Alto 1784
Sierra de las Nieves
4
Puerto de los Pilones
Pozo de Nieve
.1689
3
7
2
8
1650
1550
1450
1350
1250
La Alcazaba
Cañada del Cuerno
.1318
Area Recreativa Los Quejigales
.1414
Las Turquillas
.1356
1
500m
Ronda road

Route description

Start

Park near to the BBQ shack at the Area Recreativa Las Quejigales. Ride from here on the main track heading south, the way you arrived, to cross a small stream opposite the big house. Go as far as the road junction.

1 The 'Five K Climb'

At the first junction, take the uphill track heading toward the Puerto de los Pilones, starting amongst stands of Pinsapo, before turning a corner to emerge onto a lunar landscape. The views are stunning and stopping for a photo or two is understandable.

2 Cañada del Cuerno marker

As the angle eases, a large antenna comes into view on the horizon. A small wooden post arrives marking the start of a zig-zagging trail falling off to your left. Ignore it for now, but make a mental note for your return. Continue up toward the skyline for 200m.

3 Puerto de los Pilones

Stop at the Puerto de los Pilones panorama board. From here you can look across the ancient Quejigos (oak trees repeatedly chopped back by charcoal burners from Las Quejigales) toward Torrecilla. Our trail takes the perfect singletrack to the left of the sign starting at the first of many wooden marker poles.

4 Pozo de Nieve

'Take five' at the Pozo de Nieve, where snow was collected and turned to ice, to supply as far afield as Malaga right up until 1931. Continue on the marked trail with the occasional short difficult section. Thread in and out of rocky rises until you descend to the base of a small cliff with a spring and a water trough – the Pilar de Tolox.

5 Pilar de Tolox

This is about as far as your bikes can go. Stop here for a drink and survey the summit way above you and the shrine closer to hand. Carry on by foot for a short distance to a junction at the base of the summit slopes.

At the junction turn right and follow the marked path to the top of the mountain.

6 Torrecilla summit

1918m below you is the Mediterranean. In the distance, Morocco and the Sierras fall away all around you. Retrace your steps back to where you stashed your wheels and double back all the way to the Puerto de los Pilones.

7 Puerto de los Pilones

Emerge leftwards onto the dirtrack and roll downhill for 200m until the wooden marker post you carefully remembered earlier at Wapoint 3.

8 Cañada de Cuerno

Cascade down the tightly stacked zig-zags initially on open slopes. The trail then dives into the Pinsapo forest and the route gets increasingly tricky. Toboggan down switchback after switchback, some rocky, some rooty until eventually the angle eases at the bottom and the trail gets smoother. Merge onto the main track and pedal easily leftwards back to the start.

Time for 'tea and medals'.

Summary

Istan is a popular tourist destination which somehow manages to keep the right side of chocolate box. Surrounded by stunning mountains and the beautiful Embalse de la Conception reservoir, and packed with as many natural springs as bars and restaurants, it's a great place to spend an hour or two. This assemblage of trails is the perfect leg stretcher and ideal first route in the area.

The ride keeps to dirt tracks and combines the best viewpoints from several of the local marked trails to make the most of the town's waymarked tracks. There are information boards in the car park showing other linear routes if you want to return to the area.

A couple more nice routes to do, would be to link this route with 'Ruta 5', for a paddle in the Rio Verde, or to ride 'Ruta 4 - Castano Santo' as far as the junction with 'The Big One' (Route

Istan 

Classic 

Moderate 

12 km 

350 m 

1 - 2 hrs 

Parque Natural Sierra de Las Nieves 1:40000 

No 15, WP 11) and then on down to Marbella. Don't try to follow the waymarked local footpaths on a bike, though, as they really aren't rideable (as we found to our cost as we dangled from a wire with one hand, bike in the other on a cliff 30ft above the reservoir in the name of research!).

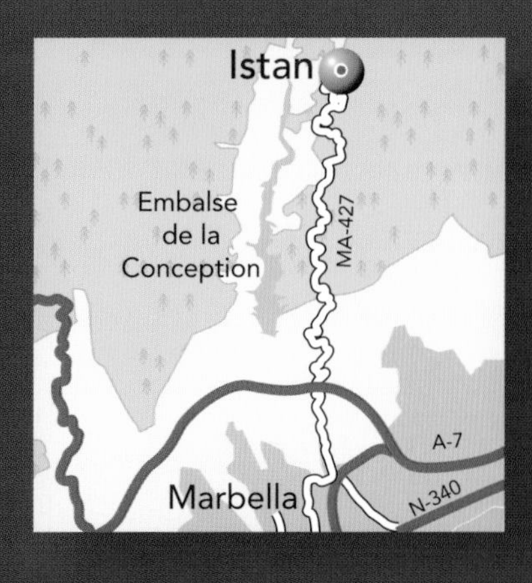

Getting there

Leave the N340 coast road near Marbella and Puerto Banus at KM marker 176 and take the winding A7176 (also marked as MA-427 and A-6206 on some maps) uphill to Istan passing the Embalse de la Conception reservoir on your left. As you enter the village, the road splits. Take the right hand fork uphill toward the car park on the edge of town.

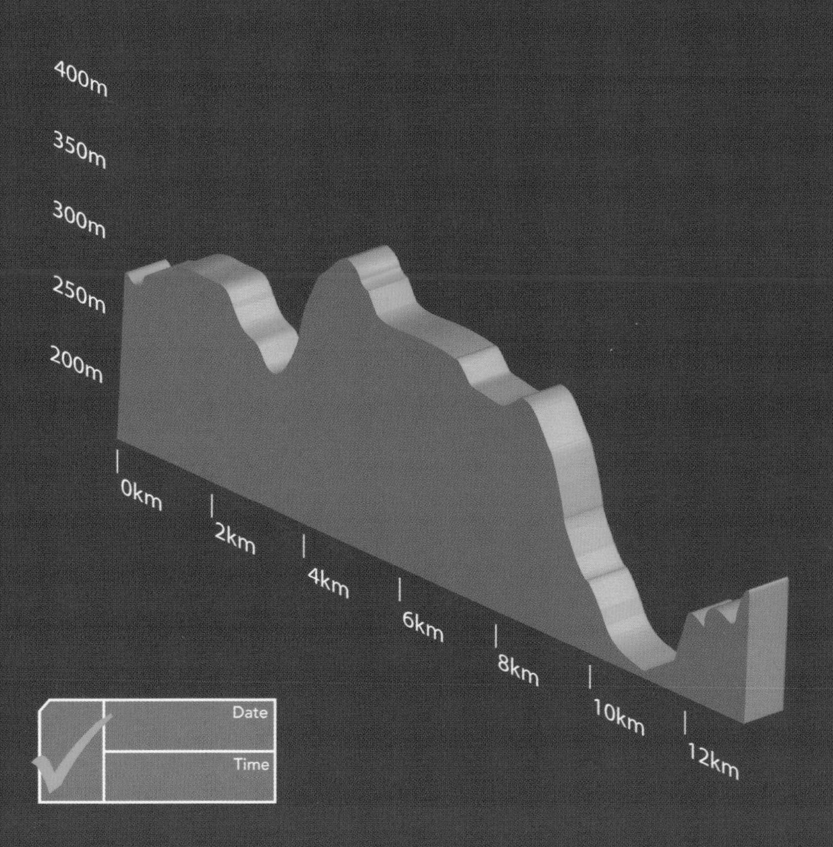

N
400
300
200
500
600
700
.502
Hoya
del
Real
.210
Avocado Trees
.356
.262
Rio Verde
.252
Istan
.309
Hotel Alto de Istan
El Nacimiento
.381
.302
Ermita de
San Miguel
Picnic Area
.329
Embalse de la
Concepcion
Marbella
500m
1
2
3
4
5
6
7
8
9

Route description

Start

From the car park, head downhill for 100m or so until you see 'El Chorro', an old watering hole used by the villagers for collecting drinking water and washing in days gone by. Fill up your Camelbak, and head back up to the car park.

1 Parking

Leave the parking area on the road heading back down toward Marbella. After 3.1km (or about 800m after the KM12 marker) leave the road at a large layby on the left opposite a 'No overtaking' sign.

2 Ermita San Miguel

Nestling in the cliff is the Ermita San Miguel. Follow the lefthand dirtrack uphill, zig-zagging through the picnic area.

3 Picnic spot

Bear right at the track at the top. Don't forget to look over your shoulder to the magnificent views across the lake towards Marbella and the Mediterranean.

4 Junction

A few metres further on, you reach a waymarked T junction. Turn left leading back toward Istan. Just above the Hotel Alto de Istan, the track forks next to a white 'Deposito de Agua' (water collection). Head downhill to your left for 200m.

5 Football pitch

Switchback right onto another track following the waymarked routes toward the Nacimiento

6 El Nacimiento

Stop for a drink and catch the view back toward Istan. Continue on the same track as it traverses around the hillside.

7 Fork in track

2.9km after El Nacimiento reach a concrete paved fork in the track and wooden marker post. Ride downhill to the left following 'Rutas 3,4,5,6'. Continue until the obvious electricity pylon.

8 Pylon

Turn back leftwards toward the village at the signposted junction. At the bottom, fork left passing through avocado orchards (and you throught they came from some exotic jungle somewhere miles away). Cross the ford and climb back into Istan.

9 'City Limits'

Navigate the maze of streets via the main square and the El Chorro spring back to the parking spot, or stop in the village for a well deserved drink.

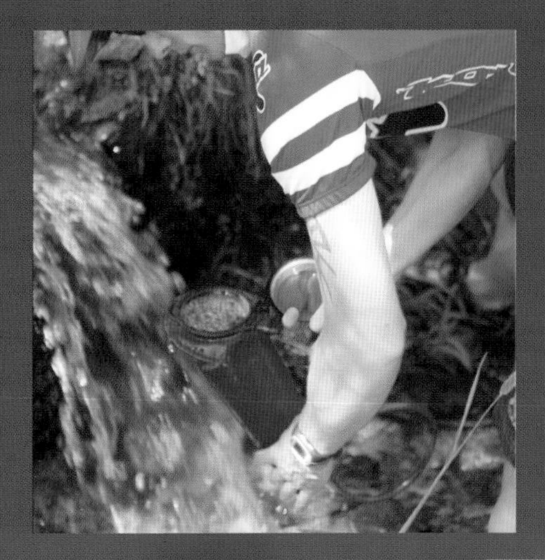

Summary

Ride from the moonscape of the Sierra de las Nieves to the sprawling metropolis of Marbella. This big but laid-back route takes a medieval 'camino' that once linked Ronda with the Mediterranean.

Starting with a long, steady climb up to the Puerto de Robledal at an altitude of nearly 1300m, before dropping down the 28kms to the coast, you'll pass from the high mountain limestone passes of the Ronda road, through lush pines and cork oaks to arrive in the crazyness of the costa a few hours later. This really is a route of contrasts.

As this is a linear route, you'll need a couple of vehicles or a sympathetic driver. Turning this into a loop means riding the extra 30km up the Ronda road. Good luck to the enduro addicts out there, if the hill doesn't get you, the traffic will!

Start 

Classic 

Easy 

36km 

1277 m

3 - 4 hrs 

Sierra de las Nieves 1:40,000 

Getting there

From the coast:

Head along the N-340 (keeping off the Peaje) until you reach San Pedro de Alcantara. At the roundabout, take the A-473 inland toward Ronda. Carry on this road until a you see 'PuntoCash' and a petrol station on a roundabout. Carry on to th e next roundabout. To the right is a large sign for the 'La Quinta' golf complex. Park up a vehicle here (this is the end of the route). Carry on driving up the Ronda road until a little after the KM14 marker you see a signposted turning on your right for Conejeras and Las Quejigales. Another 1km brings you to the start point at an isolated group of bars and restaurants on the left.

From Ronda:

Leave Ronda on the A-473 heading south to San Pedro and Marbella. Stash a car at the bottom of the road, (the La Quinta roundabout about 3km short of the N340 junction is a good place for this) and then retrace your track back up the road to the start of the trail following the directions above.

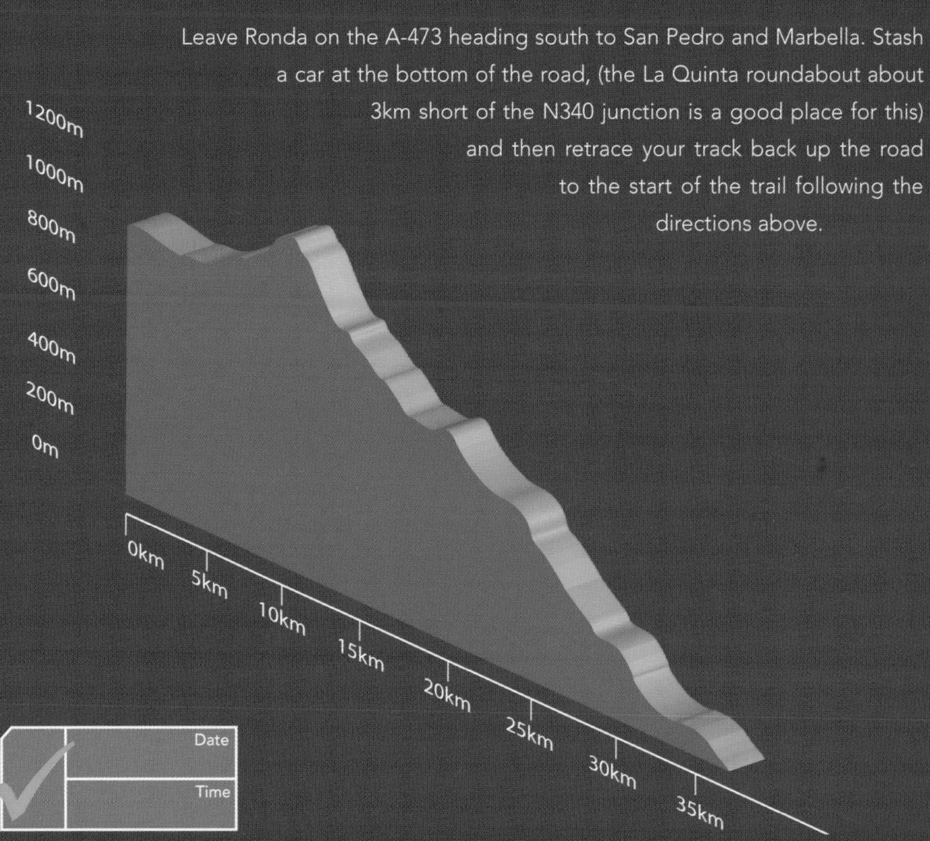

Date

Time

Route description

Start

At the top of the pass, there are a group of cafes on the side of the road called Bar La Raja and Pension El Navasillo. There is plenty of parking here. Leave your car, refuel yourselves with a coffee and bocadillo and head off!

1 Cafes

Leave the parking area and ride southwards toward Marbella. Take care on this busy road.

2 Entrance to Sierra de Las Nieves

After 1km of riding, you will see a large green 'Sierra de las Nieves' sign on your left. Turn off the road here and ride along the track past the map board, picnic area and old campground of Las Conejeras.

3 Las Quejigales junction

Here the track splits with our way to the right on the riverbank and signposted 'La Fuenfria'. The 'Puerto del Robledal', your highpoint is five kilometres further on.

4 Boca de Fuenfria

The valley opens out at the 'Boca de Fuenfria', revealing a farm on the plain on your right and an inviting looking track also heading rightwards. Ignore both and carry on the left hand side of the valley. Aim for the pass straight ahead.

5 Ruined cortijo

At the head of the valley is the ruined Corjito de la Fuenfria. Cross the babbling brook, heading for a white hut and a little fuente spilling into the stream. Climb up the track, keeping the stream on your right.

6 Junction

After 50m, turn left on the traversing dirt track, heading away from the stream. Soon the track begins to rise more steeply as the views open out back down the valley. Gasp your way upwards to the pass.

7 Puerto del Robledal

(Puerto de Trincheruelas on the IGN map). This is the highpoint of the route at 1279m. Stop for a breather and the view before continuing straight ahead. The route traverses for a while reaching another pass; the Puerto del Algarrobo.

From the pass plunge steeply down to the left on dirt track switchbacks to the junction visible below you. From here onwards, there are many minor junctions off to both sides. Ignore them all; this route takes the obvious main track all the way down to the start of civilisation on the outskirts of Marbella.

8 Las Charcas junction

Blast your way past the turning, heading back to your right and carry on round the mountain side. Before long the first cork oaks will start to line the track. These offer welcome shade for most of the way down from here. Concentrate on the track, but don't miss out on the views across the valley to the south (at 1918m, Torecelli is the highest peak in Malaga Province) and the Rio Verde valley below.

9 Puerto de la Refriega

Here the camino splits into three. Take the right hand branch, following the track down into the lush valley with the odd isolated farmhouse. Cross a few streams (some flow year round for a quick cool down) and keep on descending.

Maps

The 1:40000 Park Natural Sierra de las Nieves (published by Editorial Penibetica) covers the northern part of the route until WP11.

To cover the whole route you will need a combination of maps.

Igualeja 1065-I,

Istan 1065-II,

Marbella 1065-IV

(10) Castano Santo de Istan

A wooden marker post indicates a junction with a track to the left. Just a little way down this offshoot is the famous 'Castano Santo de Istan' - an enormous chestnut tree estimated to be over 600 years old.

Legend has it that the troops of Felipe II celebrated mass under the tree before storming the nearby Pico de Armas during the Moorish rebellion of 1570. Take a breather here, before regaining the main track to continue our descent to Marbella.

(11) Signpost to Istan

Another bike route heading round to the left to the pueblo of Istan is marked at this junction by a wooden marker post. Ignore it and carry on past the viewpoint up to the right. The landscape becomes increasingly scrubby as you roll downwards. Use 'the force' to keep to the main track. There's loads of minor junctions to ignore until you finally drop down to the river.

(12) River crossing

Turn left to cross the river on the tarmac bridge. Ride along the road keeping the golf course on your right.

(13) La Quinta

Emerge into classic Costa suburbia at the entrance to 'La Quinta' golf resort. Turn right, climbing to a roundabout. Follow the signs for the N-340 and San Pedro. Cross the motorway and pedal some more until you emerge at the roundabout where, if it's all gone to plan, your car will be waiting...

Las Alpujarras

Section 5

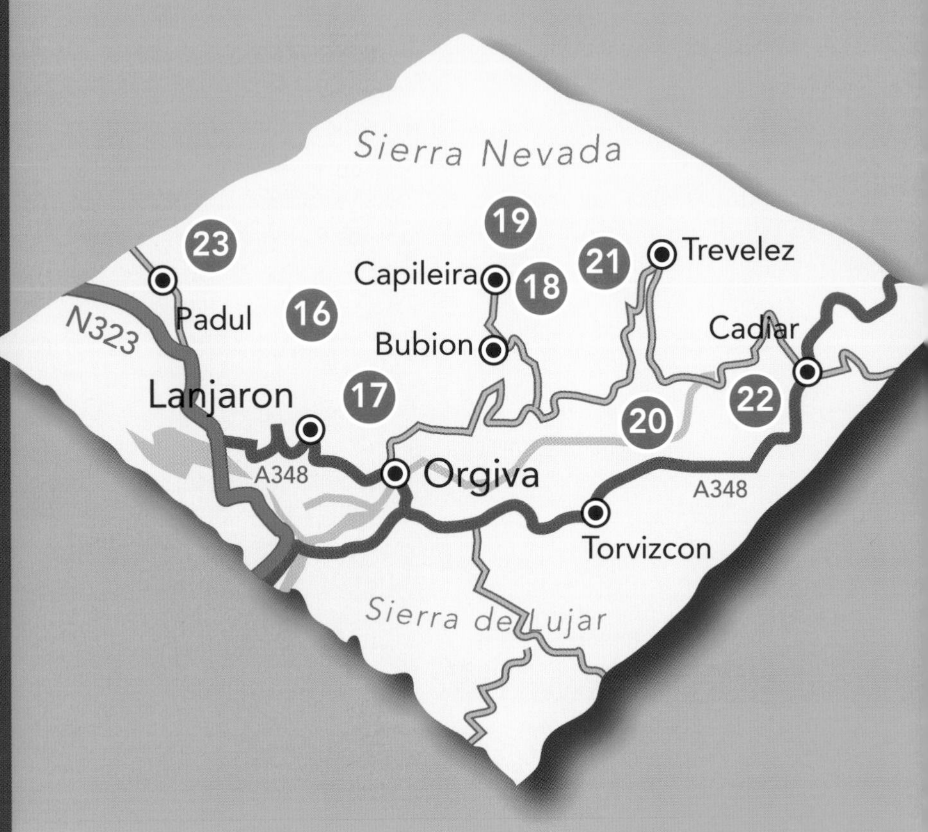

Tello Descent	16	XC
Le Rabiete	17	XC/DH
Bubion Singletrack	18	XC / DH
Angel Descent	19	XC
Busquistar Zigsags	20	XC / DH
Trevelez	21	XC
Ruta Medieval	22	XC

Introduction

Big hills, killer descents and quaint white-washed villages are the hallmarks of the southern slopes of the high Sierra Nevada, known locally as the 'Alpujarras'. Descents are long and technical, and it's no exaggeration to say that some of the best descents in the world are to be found in this region. For many, both XC and DH riders, this is the perfect year round riding holiday.

Trails can be rocky and steep, linked by good dirt tracks making for straightforward ascents and descents that are beyond awesome. Depending on your preference, you can go for long days putting together section after section of perfect descents to make up awesome XC loops, or session the descents for unlimited DH action.

If you're going out as a big group it pays to hire a couple of vehicles; this way when the big climbs all get a bit too much, you can do shuttle runs. As well, as this if you've got your own transport many of the rides can be done as linear XC routes or DH blasts.

Getting there

Easyjet, Ryanair and Monarch as well as a host of other schedule flights fly into Malaga and Granada. Malaga is a 2 hour drive with Granada being just 45 minutes from most of the area.

To get there from Malaga

Once out of the airport follow signs for Granada and Motril. At the time of writing, the motorway isn't quite finished yet and ends abruptly at Salobrena. From here stay with the signs for Granada. Pass through an unmissable huge rock gorge and soon after look out for

the turn off to Lanjaron and 'Las Alpujarras'. Turn right to Lanjaron and wind your way up the road and into the hills.

To get there from Granada

From the airport follow the A92 towards Granada. As you enter Granada take the N323 motorway towards Motril. Pass Padul and Durcal and leave the motorway at Beznar going in the direction of, Lanjaron and Las Alpujarras. Continue along this road until you reach your destination.

Where to stay

The towns of Lanjaron and Orgiva make good valley bases. Being at a lower altitude, they don't tend to be quite so cold in the winter months. Lanjaron is known for its therapeutic waters and is quite genteel, whilst Orgiva is far more of a bustling local metropolis. Small hotels, pensions and self-catering accommodation is easily found by a search on the web for accommodation in Andalucia or the Alpujarras. There is also a very pleasant campsite just on the edge of Orgiva and what is billed as the 'highest campsite' up at 1400m in Trevelez (not recommended for a winter visit!).

Higher up the mountain, any of the small white washed villages, including Bubion, Capileira and Pampaneira, allow for a quick start on the higher trails. In Bubion, Hostal Las Terrazas, www.terrazasalpujarra.com, provides comfortable accommodation at very reasonable prices, and also has apartments to rent. Just up the road in Capileira, the Hostal Rural Apalaya; www.hostalatalaya.com, also has comfortable hostal accommodation and cottages to let.

Nevada Active and Freeride Spain also have cottages and apartments to let.

Food & drink

This area also has no shortage of good bars and eateries. In Bubion try 'El Artesia' or 'Los Culpables' for food (both on the main street). In Lanjaron, several english speaking bars dot the high street, including 'Bar Health', well known for its good old fashioned English fried breakfast! At the western end of Lanjaron is the 'Terrasse Bar' which has excellent tapas and friendly local service. The ice cream parlour in the centre of Lanjaron is however where all the real locals hang out.

For those self catering there are a couple of small supermarkets in Bubion and Capileira, and slightly larger ones in Orgiva and Lanjaron. If you are self catering, though, it's worth a stop at one of the big supermarkets alongside the motorway en route from the airport.

This area is famous for it's ham. Everywhere you go you will see huge hams, hanging up to cure in the mountain air and locals from Malaga and Granada will come out to this area for a weekend break just to buy a ham. You know you've just got to try some.

Maps

The Series Alpina Sierra Nevada map is the best map to get hold of and can easily be bought at a variety of shops in the villages of Bubion and Capileira, as well as in the petrol station on the main road outside Pampaneira.

Bike shops & services

Despite the awesomness of the riding in the area, the locals haven't really switched on to mountain biking yet, and as a result genuine mountain bike shops are a bit rare hereabouts. Take any spares you might need with you as the nearest big bike shop is in Granada, though there is a small shop recently opened in Durcal.

If you're not planning on a DIY trip, there are now quite a few British and English speaking guiding outfits in the area. Freeride Spain operate out of Lanjaron and specialise in good technical XC riding, whilst Switchbacks, based in Bubion, is popular with DH riders and does vehicle uplift. Both companies provide excellent professional guiding service, accommodation and have a wealth of local knowledge. Also based in Padul is Nevada Acitve who can give advice on both road and mountain bike riding and have bikes for hire.

STACK
Wobble
Flop
www.freeridespain.com
0034 958772082
CALL
FULL OF GOODNESS

Tello Descent

Summary

The Tello descent, as the route is known locally, follows a traditional mule trail down the steep sided Rio de Lanjaron. A somewhat gruelling ascent is paid back with one of the best all out cobbled, switchbacked descents in the area. The fun just never stops from top to bottom, and as the terrain varies under wheel from section to section, you just have to keep on working for it. From technical to flowing, scenic to sensational, this is a route that just keeps on giving right to the very last cactus!

The ride is long and and the descent technical. Even on the all out downhill sections, you'll find yourself stopping just to catch your breath now and again, but it's such a fine ride that if you do manage to beg, steal or borrow a lift up to the top, you're bound to find yourself on the trail more than once in your lifetime.

Aguas de Lanjaron

Epic

Extreme

27 km

1155 m

4 - 5 hrs

Editorial Alpina Sierra Nevada

Getting there

The small spa town of Lanjaron is situated at the gateway to the Alpujarras on the A348. From the west and the motorway (N322), take the turn off signposted Lanjaron, and follow the road for approximately 10km to reach the edge of town.

From the east (Bubion), follow the A4130 towards Granada. Turn right at the junction at Orgiva and continue on the A348 for 8km to Lanjaron.

Start point

Park on the roadside as you head west out of Lanjaron towards Granada. Continue along this road until you see a large building with 'Aguas Lanjaron' painted on it. On the lefthand side of the 'Aguas Lanjaron' is a steep road heading upwards. Follow this and you'll soon see a sign for 'Parque Natural' and smaller signs for 'Tello'.

Before long the park road turns into a wide dirt track which winds steadily uphill. This is the only road you need to follow until you start the descent. Whenever you come to a junction, head in the direction of 'Tello'.

1700m
1500m
1300m
1100m
900m
700m

0km
5km
10km
15km
20km
25km

Date
Time

XC

N
1700
1600
1500
1400
1300
1200
El Vadillo
Tello
Hoya
del Pedregal
Weather Station
Fuente
Pedro Calvo
GR7
Acequia Alta
Bordaila
Rio Lanjaron
El Almendral
Acequia Mesqueri
GR7
Aguas de Lanjaron
Cerro de
la Escolta
.949
.804
To Granada
Lanjaron
.576
.8
C-333
To Orgiva
1km
1
2
3
4
5
6
7

Route description

1 Pedro Calvo Fuente 1200m

Just over half way up the ascent, the Pedro Calvo water fountain makes a welcome break. This is to be found on a bend in the track and just 10 metres off the main track to the left. From here it's onwards and upwards.

2 Track junction 1625m

Shortly after a fenced off weather station, a narrower track appears on the right (sign to 'Tello' on the junction). Turn right here and lose some height as you start to descend into the back of the valley. At a small fork go right, and at the end of this track a red and white post marker indicates the start of the singletrack.

3 Exposed traverse

A sensational and exposed piece of singletrack clings precariously to the side of the hill. Riding this, there are times when you won't want to look down. Eventually the narrow path starts swinging around a few switchbacks to emerge in a big open area. Here the trail heads right dropping abruptly down steep dirt, reminiscent of Morzine, into a wooded area with a ruined building. This is Casa Forestal de Tello and recently ravaged by forest fires the trail is not immediately apparent.

4 Ruined building

Go left from the ruin, through an area of fallen trees and sniff out a vague line of dirt to a couple of switchbacks over a water channel. This leads to an old low bridge over the river at the bottom of the valley.

From the bridge, a short hike upwards takes you past a small building. Five minutes later you are back on your bike and riding delightful flowing singletrack.

5 Building, junction and collection of signs

A collection of signs at the base of a huge tree point in a bewildering assortment of directions. Head rightwards, following the sign to 'Lanjaron 5km', starting off on a wide path lined by huge chestnut trees. As you progress, chunky rocks, cobbles, rock steps and tight switchbacks come at you in every combination.

6 Junction with red X's

Arrive at a junction (just after a house and a fence) where a metal gate post on the right has a vague red X, denoting no access, as does the track on the left with an X painted on the rock on the track itself. Look in front of you and below the track to see where the trail continues off leftwards.

Expect more of the same with rocks, tight switchbacks, cobbled berms and boulder drops. After a while the trail eases and becomes smooth, to eventually brings you into a long exposed traverse above the valley. Drop steeply out of this onto a track junction.

7 Track junction

Turn right down a wide dirt track There are a couple of right hand turn offs off this, but ignore these and instead look for a similar trail dropping off to the right. The final section of trail inevitably takes you down another steep cobbled path with very tight switchbacks, passing some huge photogenic cactuses en route, to at last deposit you exhausted and grinning at the bottom.

Now wasn't that hill climb worth it?

bikefaX

The Rabiete Blast

17 Las Alpujarras

Summary

Between the outskirts of Lanjaron and the suburbs of Orgiva lies a blast of a route. When you just can't face another big day out, but also can't bear not to get at least some dirt underneath your wheels, then the short blast down the southerly slopes of Cerro Mimbre, passing the rocky outcrop of the Rabiete will more than satisfy both desires.

The tight switchbacks around the Rabiete combine with the odd tricky manoeuvre as you try to keep it together in the ruts and stay out of the shrubbery en route to the river. One last steep dusty drop takes you into the olive groves and down to the river.

At the bottom of the hill the easy track takes you down the banks of the Rio Chico and out into Orgiva.

The route itself is 6km with a further 6km for the return leg on the road.

Lanjaron 

Blast 

Grade 3

12 km 

450 m 

1 -2 hrs 

Editorial Alpina
Sierra Nevada 

Getting there

The small spa town of Lanjaron is situated at the gateway to the Alpujarras on the A348. From the west and the motorway (N322), take the turn off signposted 'Lanjaron', and follow the road for approximately 10km to reach the edge of town.

From the east (Bubion), follow the A4130 towards Granada. Turn right at the junction at Orgiva and continue on the A348 for 8km to Lanjaron.

Start point

Just outside Lanjaron, on the road heading eastwards out of town towards Orgiva, is a steep tarmac road on the left. The road is signposted to a campsite and 'Caballo Blanco' Horse Centre. Fifty metres on from this is a large parking bay on the side of the road.

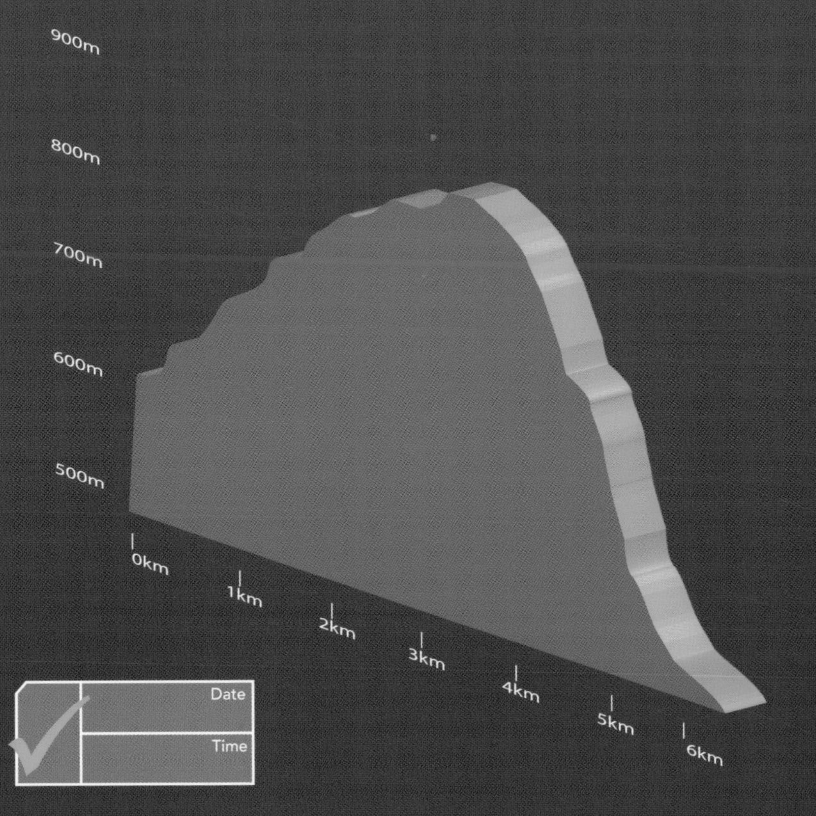

Date

Time

N
To Orgiva
3
4
Rio Sucio
600
800
700
2
Rabiete
693
Cortijo de
los Meridas
900
1000
GR7
C-333
.629
Cerro
Mimbre
1072
1
.911
El Colmenar
GR7
Cortijo de
Vista Alegre
.929
.694
P
Tello
Descent
1km
Lanjaron
.666

Route description

Start

Pedal steeply uphill for about 20 minutes, until you go under a small bridge and arrive at a flat area overlooking the valley. You'll notice the 'Caballo Blanco' sign pointing right. Ignore this and after a brief rest for breath, head off left continuing on the main concrete track.

Pass one junction with a track going off leftwards and continue riding as far as a large wooden GR142 signpost on the right of the track.

1 GR142 signpost

Follow the trail signposted 'Orgiva 1hr'. Starting off on a flattish section, you'll first be picking a line through large rocks, then as the gradient soon drops and you'll find yourself flying down a fine flowing section of trail. Try not to get too carried away though, as technical rocky sections seem to pop out of nowhere.

2 The Rabiete

After a way the trail suddenly drops steeply to squeeze you into some real tricky rut and rock filled sections.

From here on in the rocks ease off but are replaced by ruts galore as the path becomes exceedingly worn, with many new lines forming around old ones that have become eroded with the rain. It is easy to see why this section of trail is so worn as it's almost impossible not to skid on the steep loose surface. Make your way down trying to stay out of the grooves.

At the end of the ruts a steep drop takes you over the brow. Just hang on to the bottom for a nice run out into olive groves and fields. Just after the last bit of steep dirt, the trail seems to disappear at the top of a big cliff. Go right to pick up a track which snakes back around to underneath the cliff, and breathe a sigh of relief as you reach the dirt track.

3 Dirt track

Follow this track down the hill with loads of fun little jumps off the drainage channels. Ignore any junctions until you hit the road at the top end of Orgiva. Take a breather and prepare yourself for the short haul back up to your car.

4 Road

Turn right onto the road and gradually make your way uphill for 5km back to Lanjaron.

Summary

Utilising an old footpath on the slopes of the mountain side just below the National Park, the Bubion switchbacks offer everything you could ever want from a trail.

Starting out open and loose, it's a struggle not to wash out on some of the corners. Further down take care as you cross and recross the ascent road several times. Between the roads, sections vary from 'take a deep breath' steep to laid back and earthy.

The final section of deep, gully like switchbacks under huge ancient trees spits you out onto the old cobblestoned path and into the middle of the whitewashed village of Bubion.

This is also a great piece of trail to go and find if you've only got half a day to spare.

Capileira 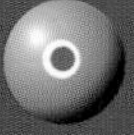

Expert 

Hard 

16 km

700 m 

2 - 3 hrs 

Editorial Alpina Sierra Nevada 

Getting there

To get to Capileira, follow the A4130 (from Orgiva or Trevelez) as far as Pampaneira. If coming from Orgiva turn left at the junction opposite the petrol station. Continue up the hill and through the village of Bubion to arrive in Capileira.

If coming from Trevelez direction, the petrol station and junction are on the right, 3km after passing through Pitres.

Start point

Park your car either in the village of Capileira itself or just above the village on the side of the road. Not too far up though, as some poor soul is going to have to pedal back up here for the car.

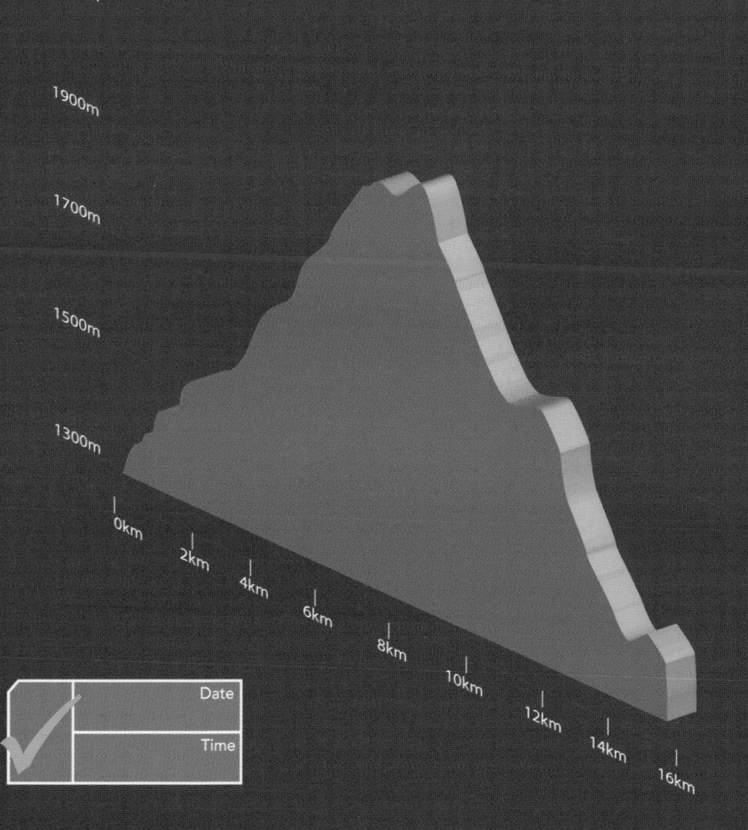

Date

Time

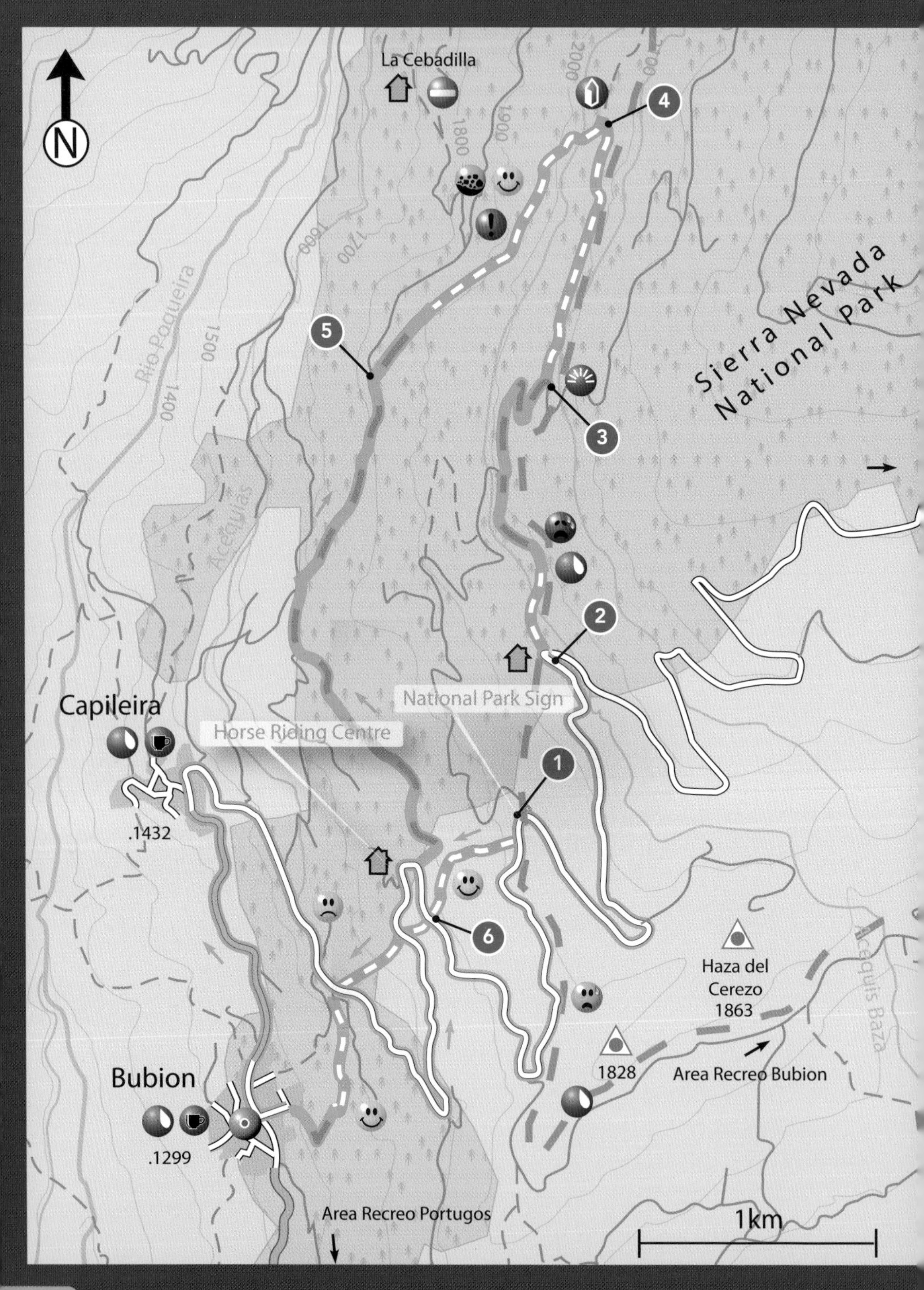
N
La Cebadilla
2000
2100
1900
1800
1700
1600
1500
1400
Rio Poqueira
Acequias
Sierra Nevada
National Park
National Park Sign
Horse Riding Centre
Capileira
.1432
Bubion
.1299
Haza del
Cerezo
1863
1828
Area Recreo Bubion
Acequis Baza
Area Recreo Portugos
1km
1
2
3
4
5
6

Route description

Start

From Capileira continue on up the rough tarmac road heading for 'Area Recreativa Hoya Portillo'. As you toil upwards you get glimpses of your final descent as the singletrack repeatedly cuts across the road. Keep going though, it'll be worth it.

1 Sierra Nevada National Park sign

Go left staying on the main track until the next large righthand bend.

2 House on left / Track 1960m

On the big righthand bend of the main track, next to the small farm of 'Casa Grande', a narrow dirt track goes off left. Take this until it joins up with a wider dirt track which zigzags uphill. Follow the track uphill for 700m until, on a bend, you see thin singletrack going up onto a small viewpoint. Go to the top of this, and just over the other side the trail becomes more obvious as it disappears into the distance.

3 Viewpoint & start of singletrack

From the viewpoint follow the narrow snaking singletrack as its threads its way around the hillside. Enjoy the slim weaving line as it undulates onwards. A few occasional dips and rises remind you that it's not quite all downhill yet. Ride as far as a fork in the trail where at a signpost the path doubles back on itself.

4 Signpost

A wooden signpost points left to 'Acequia de Poqueira'. This is a great trail section; narrow, fast and flowing, but watch out for a small landslip just after a set of tight switchbacks. Towards the end, the path widens into a loose, slightly off camber double track, dropping you onto a wide track in the forest.

5 Forest track

Turn left and peddle easily to the road junction next to the Horse Centre. This is the road up which you ascended earlier. Turn left to go uphill briefly, until you see red and white marker posts pointing you down a path on the right.

6 Singletrack

This is the start of an awesome descent which takes you all the way back to Bubion. Crossing the ascent road several times, the riding is steep and technical with loads of twists and turns, and tight little switchbacks. The final section takes you racing past fields and houses, and finally down a concrete path right into the middle of the village.

At the bottom, volunteer one person to ride the final 2 kilometres back up the hill to fetch the car whilst everyone else chills out at one of Bubion's many roadside bars.

Options

If you can find a driver, this is a great piece of trail to do again and again. To do this drive up the road as far as a big bend next to the big Sierra Nevada Park sign. Park here and ride back down the road for about 50m to the start of the singletrack. The start is a little vague, but you can just make out a thin line of dirt working its way through the small bushes. Watch out for it disappearing rightwards at the first firebreak. After this the line is obvious and it just gets better and better. The descent takes just about the same amount of time as it takes a car to drive back down.

Summary

Starting high up on the very edge of the National Park is a trail worthy of at least 5 stars in any book. Earthy singletrack, rocky switchbacks and even a quaint Spanish village where you ride through tiny whitewashed streets.

The route is blessed with three iconic sections of singletrack, each with its own individual character. Put together, they make up one of the finest routes in the mountains.

The descent starts with a fast tight section of dusty switchbacks. Follow this with flowing earthy singletrack and finish with a rocky vertigo inducing finale to finish right in the heart of the village. And like any perfect ride, the route starts with coffees in Capileira and finishes with beers in Bubion.

Like all the rides hereabouts it does start with a big ascent so if you've got a big rig, you may want to arrange a lift at least part way. Allow 2 hours for the ascent.

Capileira 

Epic 

Extreme 

25 km 

900 m 

5 - 7 hrs 

Editorial Alpina Sierra Nevada 

Getting there

To get to Capileira, follow the A4130 (from Orgiva or Trevelez) as far as Pampaneira. If coming from Orgiva turn left at the junction opposite the petrol station and continue up the hill and through the village of Bubion to arrive in Capileira.

If coming from Trevelez direction, the petrol station and junction are on the right 3km after passing through Pitres.

Start point

Park in any of the carparks in the village of Capileira and head up the road and out of the village towards the Sierra Nevada National Park.

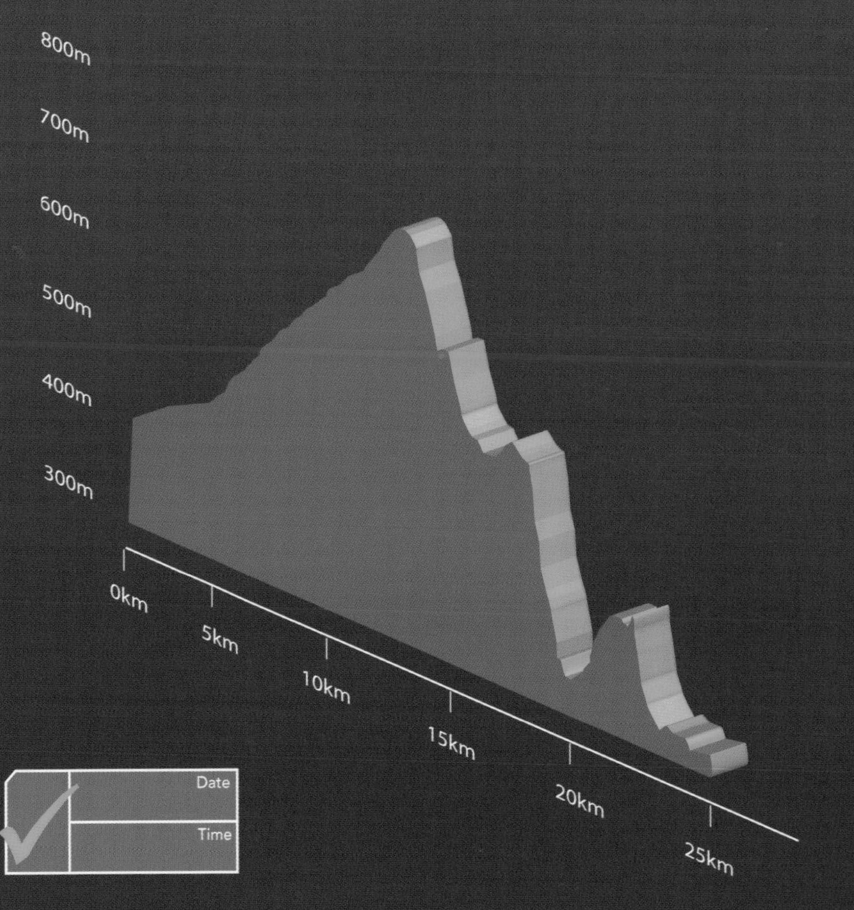

Date

Time

N
Sierra Nevada
National Park
Pitres
Capilerilla
Haza
del Cerezo
El Monte
Picon
del Monte
1828
Recreo Bubion
National Park
Sign
To Area
Recreo Portugos
.1524
.1609
Horse Riding
Centre
Penon
Angel
Bubion
Pampaniera
.1432
Capileira
1km
Acequia Baja
2000
1800
1700
1600
1500
1400
1
2
3
4
5
6
7
8

Route description

Start

From Capileira head up the road out of the village. The rough tarmac road zigzags its way up the hill, heading for the National Park Centre at Area Recreativa Hoya del Portillo, at the lofty altitude of 2150m.

Stay on the main route (going right) at the horse riding centre. At the next big junction, a sign points rightwards to the 'Area de Recreo de Portugos'.

1 Junction to Area Recreo Portugos

Take the little drop and jump on the bend' or just go round by the road, turning right at the junction. Pass a watering spot after approximately 1km. 600 m further on is a green sign on the right pointing to Pitres and Bubion.

2 Pitres / Bubion sign

This section of trail is just mouthwatering. Head steeply down endless switchbacks. Try not to straighline it; this is a locals' favourite trail and we'll make no friends by trashing it. At a dirt track at the bottom, when you've finished grinning and panting from the exhilaration of it all, don't put the seat back up just yet 'cos there's still more to come.

3 Stream/ track junction

From here take the track over the stream on the left, swooping down to the right initially but soon narrowing into some more lively singletrack. Watch out for the steep and technical switchbacks that are interspersed along this trail. At the bottom you'll find yourself at a vehicle track next to a wide open grass area, with a number of buildings around the edges. Follow this track down to the right until you reach a tarmac road and a sign for Capilerilla after about 400m.

4 Road/ Capilerilla sign

Follow the road to the right into the village itself. Capilerilla remains a quaint little place with funny tight little streets, as yet untouched by tourism. Make your way to the top left hand edge of the village. With a maze of narrow streets to choose from it's best to go on your instincts here, but with the village being so small it's hard to get completely lost. Before long you will find yourself at the far end of the village. Look out for the wooden signpost for the GR route, which will appear either up or down the road depending on where you exit the village.

5 Signpost 'Pitres 0.5km, Bubion 5.5km'

The sign points down the hill for Pitres and up for Bubion. Follow the track towards Bubion, making your way round to the left and traversing underneath a wall on your right. The trail soon climbs steeply up and you might find yourself pushing here for a minute or two, ride it all if you're that way inclined. Navigation can get a bit confusing here with a collection of tracks all branching off the main trail.

Continue up the main track quite steeply and take the first main vehicle track sweeping off to the left. Follow this as it narrows and takes you around a couple of hairpins until you reach a chain across the track (GR footpath coming in on right). Just above here you will find yourself at a T-junction with a major track.

6 Track

Follow this vehicle track left for 1km, climbing

gradually towards the ridgeline in front of you. Ignore any turnings off to the sides and continue until you begin heading slightly downhill and into a major junction of many tracks.

7 Major crossroads

Head straight over, following the GR route as it drops down suddenly on a wide but loose gravel track. Don't get too excited though, just as quickly as it dips downwards, it begins climbing steeply again. Continue steeply until you reach a small junction in the trails. Take the right hand trail here for a short distance until you reach yet another crossroads. Up to your right are small buildings and opposite a high barbed wire fence. Head straight over the crossroads for a short, sharp climb up to the ridge of the Pena del Angel. You'll be greeted by a fantastic view of Bubion and the valley below. Take a breather here to gawp at both the view of Bubion and the amazing singletrack dropping over the edge below.

8 Angel Descent

This last section of trail is one final sheer heart stopping descent. It's seat down and time for a non-stop, rocky, twisting and exhilarating finish into the village. There will be times when you will be asking yourself, 'Will it ever stop?!'

In the end it does, and a final fast broad path takes you straight into the middle of Bubion. From Bubion head right and uphill for just over a kilometre to get back to Capileira, or send one poor soul up to fetch the car whilst you enjoy beers in Bubion.

20 Las Alpujarras
Busquistar Zigzags

Summary

You'll be seeing switchbacks in your sleep after this one. The trail that crosses and re-crosses the Trevelez gorge is a must for those who love tight, technical trails and testing switchbacks. From the start point you should be able to make out at least one, if not most of the neat zigzags that give this route its character. The perfect line of the trail looks as if it has been drawn on to the exposed hillside as they form perfect Zs.

Be ready for some big climbs to compensate for these great trails. Embrace the downhiller in you and be prepared to push. On the final descent down the gorge, crank the bike right over into those corners or be prepared to walk!

The whole route feels like a big day out and is certain to leave you with weary legs and a big smile on your face.

Busquistar

Epic 

Off the scale 

25 km 

1115 m 

4 - 6 hrs

La Alpujarra. Series Alpina 

Getting there

Busquistar is situated on the A4130 between Orgiva and Trevelez.

Start Point

Park in the village of Busquistar, where there is parking on the right outside the shops, just as you turn into the village. Head out of the village on the main road towards Portugos as far as the layby and track on the left.

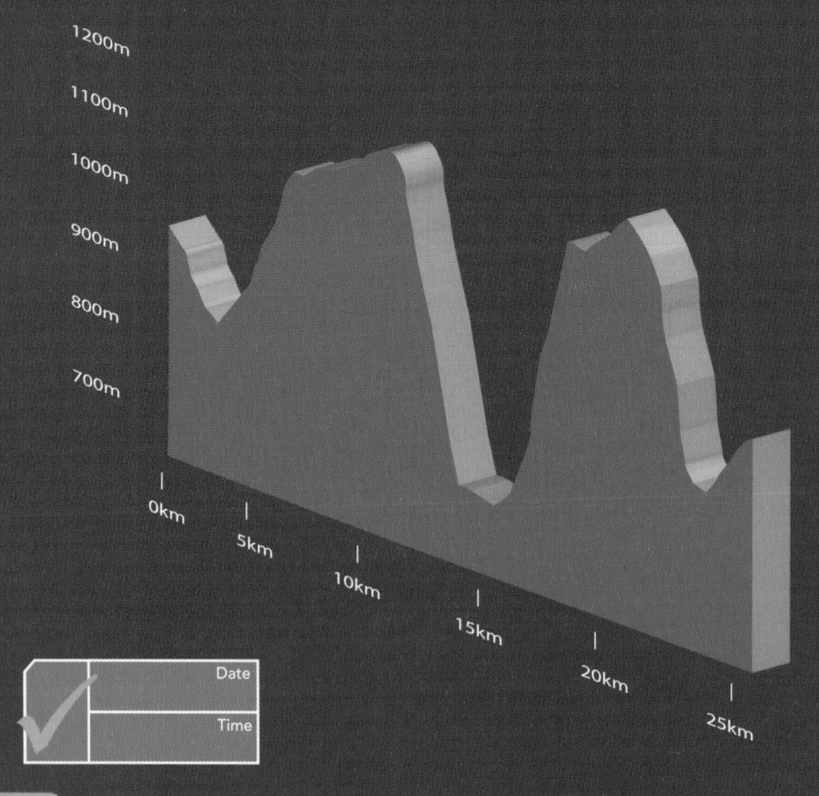

Date

Time

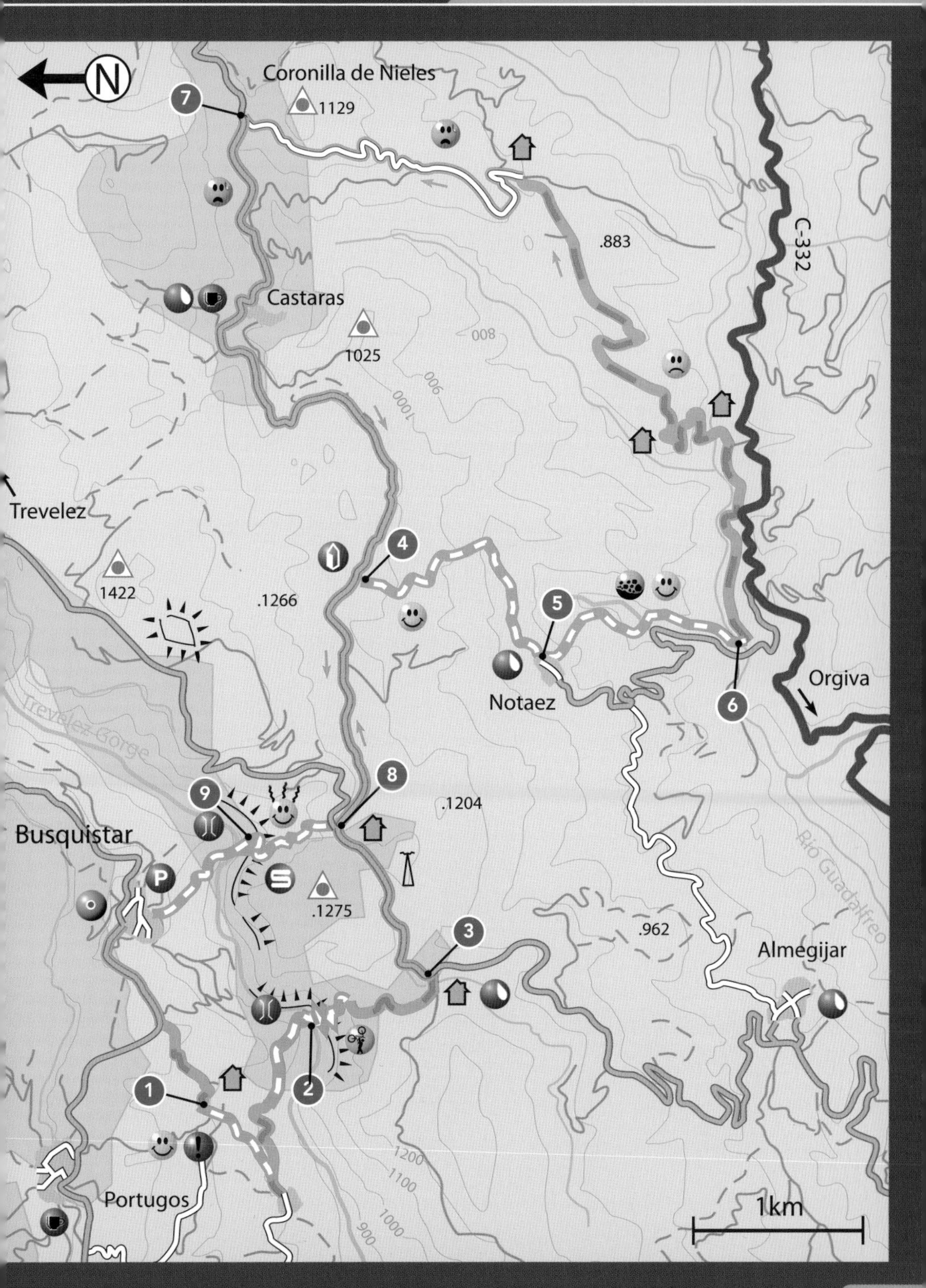

N
Coronilla de Nieles
1129
7
.883
C-332
Castaras
1025
800
900
1000
Trevelez
4
1422
.1266
5
6
Notaez
Orgiva
Trevelez Gorge
8
9
.1204
Busquistar
P
.1275
Río Guadalfeo
3
.962
Almegijar
2
1
1200
1100
Portugos
1000
900
1km

Route description

Start

About 600m out of Busquistar towards Portugos is a track bearing off left, just before a metal barrier. At the entrance to the track is a sign saying 'Mesquita de Busquistar'. Set off down the track ignoring the fork off to the right a few metres down. Carry on round a series of hairpins, stopping at the third left hand hairpin.

1 Third left hairpin

Here, look down over the edge and notice a trail disappearing off to the right underneath you. Go right and follow this as it traverses the hillside making its way over rock slabs and cobbles. After no more than 500m you will come to a junction in the trail marked by a post. Pause for a minute here and have a look at the neat zig-zag trail on the far side of the gorge. Soon enough you'll be making your way up these.

At a small gate, take the trail to the left going around a tight switchback below you. The trail continues through a series of switchbacks before straightening out again and traversing back in the opposite direction to before and descending towards the bottom of the gorge. Make your way over rocky blocks and more cobbled sections until you reach the bridge at the bottom of the gorge.

2 Bottom of the gorge

Time to push up the zig zags you were admiring from the far side of the gorge. They look a lot worse than they actually are and seem to take no time at all to push up. There are some fantastic views to be had whilst pushing up and it's great to see the layers of trail unfold beneath you. Before you know it you'll pop out at the top and arrive at an open section at the end of a grassy track. Mount the bike again and make your way along the track until you reach a collection of buildings. At the buildings turn left, and descend onto a road.

3 Road

Turn left onto the road, heading uphill briefly. Once over the brow of the hill descend gradually, soon reaching a bend in the road and a junction. Make a mental note of this junction because you will be arriving back here later in the day. Keep following the road to the right, keeping an eye out for a trail heading off to the right after about 300m.

4 GR142 Sign

The trail is marked by a red wooden sign post pointing to 'Notaez'. Take this path and enjoy descending through meadows and scrub over a variety of terrain from cobbled stuff to loose twisty trail. The trail is hard to follow in a couple of places, but with a bit of a poke about is easy to find again. Before long you find yourself reaching the top end of Notaez.

5 Notaez

Notaez is a maze of narrow streets so it is best to go on instinct here and head straight down towards the bottom of the village. It is a really picturesque place, so it may be worth taking a break here, but if you do you may find yourself being barked at by a hundred little dogs.

The trail you are looking for heads straight out of the bottom of Notaez. It is very distinct as it drops into a tight gully between fields. Later on it steepens up considerably with large loose rocks at the top and a loose surface that turns into finer gravel as you descend. The final descent takes you through huge cactuses, eventually reaching the dry river bed of the Rio Guadalfreo.

6 Rio Guadalfreo

At the river bed, cross the river (bridge or ford depending on river level) and follow the track alongside the river, upstream for 1km. Just past a deep ravine where another river comes in from the left, is a track coming down from the road on the right to cross the river and head up a steep spur on the left. Go left and zigzag steeply uphill past several 'work in progress' houses. At the top of the spur things ease a little with the track continuing at a gentler angle to the top of the hill.

7 Road to Castaras

Turn left and follow the road to the quaint mountain village of Castaras. Castaras offers the opportunity to pause for a moment and regain strength at one of the little bars, before a short ascent to the top of the second set of zigzags and the final testing descent. Once recovered from the hill pedal out of Castaras as far as the junction for Trevelez.

8 Junction/top of zig-zags

At the junction (which you passed earlier in the day) look out for a trail leading off at the corner where the two roads meet. It is marked by a red and white GR marker post. Follow the trail as it descends along fast, smooth singletrack before switching over to the other side of the gully. Soon enough it drops into cobbled switchbacks, similar to those you walked up earlier.

Hang on tight as you get shaken about, not forgetting about those sharp switchbacks. Watch out for the drops as you make your way down – take it easy, as some of them you won't recover from if you get it wrong!! At the bottom you'll find yourself at a bridge crossing the river at the bottom of the gorge.

9 Bridge

Cross the bridge and make your way up the trail, pushing at first. Shortly the gradient eases and the trail becomes semi rideable until becoming steeper again as you reach the bottom end of Busquistar. Follow your nose up through the village to find your car.

A truly memorable route.

Summary

With the aid of a driver to drop you off in Trevelez and to pick you up in Bubion, this is one of those truly great cross-country routes. Even with the aid of a lift to the start this not a ride to be taken lightly. For those who like earthy wooded singletrack, this ride is a winner. In its 25km, it manages to pack in grand descents, smooth undulating XC singletrack and of course the odd killer climb as it pops in and out of the steeply cut in gorges that bite into the hillside.

At times the perfect singletrack seems endless and it's sure to have something for everyone. The ride follows the GR7, a long distance footpath, from Trevelez all the way to Bubion and does have a sense of a journey about it. Take plenty of provisions, set off and enjoy.

There are also a fair few variations and options on this route making it a ride you could easily go back for again.

Trevelez 

Expert 

Hard 

25 km 

1150 m 

5 hrs 

Series Alpina Sierra Nevada 

Getting there

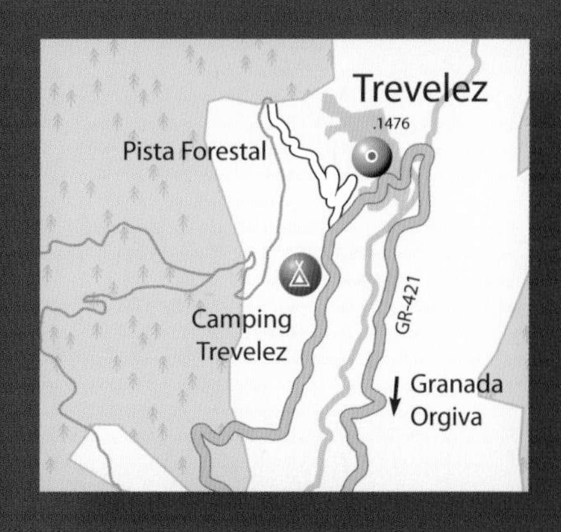

Trevelez is situated at the head of the Rio Trevelez Gorge and is 35km from Orgiva. From Orgiva take the winding A4130 through Pampaneira and Portugos.

Start point

As you approach Trevelez, you will spot 'Camping Trevelez' on the left hand side of the road. Half way between the campsite and the village is a minor road going off up the hill. Take this as far as the 'Pista Forestal'. Go up the pista, which in the main is a good wide dirt road, only one section is worryingly rough. Or if your lift doesn't want to drive up the track, park here and pedal your way steeply up hill, until just before a big right hand bend you see a large cow shed with a flat stone roof to the left of the track.

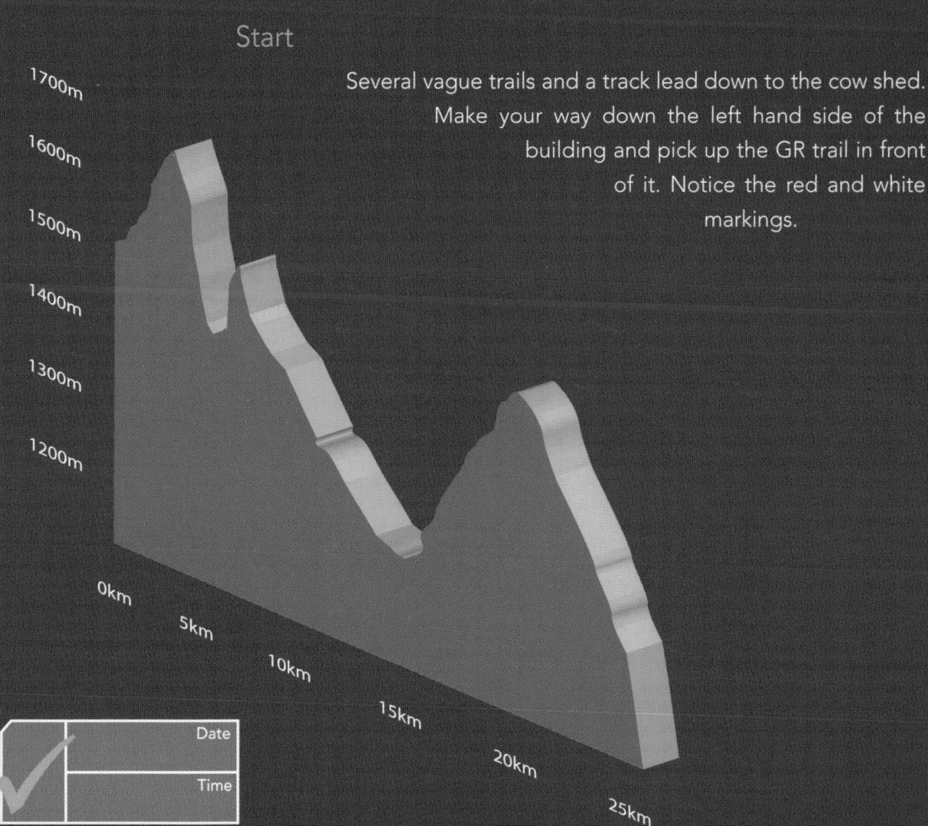

Several vague trails and a track lead down to the cow shed. Make your way down the left hand side of the building and pick up the GR trail in front of it. Notice the red and white markings.

Bubion
13
Loma del Jabali
Haza del
Cerezo
1828
2000
1900
12
To Bubion
1800
Optional Start
Capilerilla
1700
1600
11
1300
10
1500
Optional Ascent
1200
1400
Pitres
Portugos
1100
8
6
Mecina
Optional Descent
Fondales
Atalbeitar
7
9
Ferreirola
.1156
1000
1100
1200
Busquistar
Rio Trevelez
Corona
Picon
1275
.1392
Cerro d
los Prad

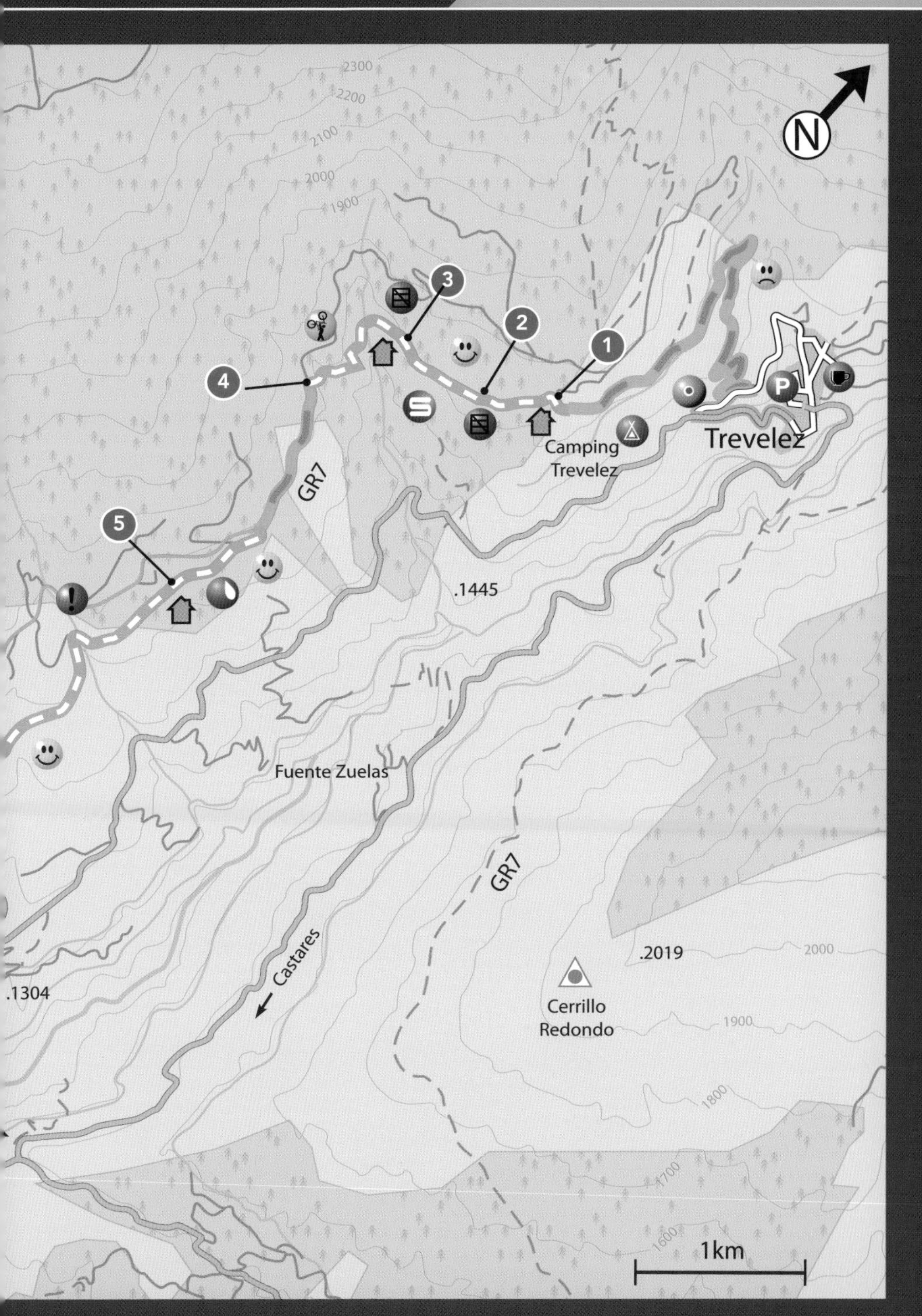
2300
2200
2100
2000
1900
N
1
2
3
4
5
GR7
Camping Trevelez
Trevelez
.1445
Fuente Zuelas
GR7
Castares
.1304
.2019
2000
Cerrillo Redondo
1900
1800
1700
1600
1km

Route description

1 Cow shed

Once past the cow shed follow the trail as it descends straight down the hill to a rickety home made gate. Go through the gate and follow the trail downwards, soon bearing off right into the trees. Follow it for a while as it reaches another gate on the far side of a riverbed. Carry on through the gate and climb for a moment. Soon the trail heads downwards again and out into the open to reach a GR signpost and a junction.

2 Switchbacks

Take the left hand trail downwards. The track descends towards the bottom of the gully through a series of tight switchbacks. Before long the path levels out and heads back in towards the gully, and up and over a few short, sharp climbs. You may find yourself pushing a couple of these. Make your way around the ruin with some amusing cracks in it, and continue to yet another gate.

3 Rustic gate

Go through the gate and descend to the river at the heart of the gully. Take a breather here to psyche yourself up for a killer push back up. This looks great to come down, but fear not, the rest of the riding more than makes up for it. Halfway up, a track cuts across the trail. Make your way straight over and back onto the GR7 to the top.

4 Vehicle track

At the top is a big dirt track with a 'Parque Natural' sign opposite. Turn left onto the track. Around the corner is a signpost and a GR trail heading up on the right. Ignore this and follow the sign for Portugos, continuing on the track for a moment. After 300m keep an eye out for a piece of singletrack and a GR marker post on your left.

Take this singletrack swooping up and down on a truly iconic piece of singletrack as far as a short steep climb up to a farm building.

5 Farm building

At the building look out for the GR markers painted on the rocks. This is the start of more 'never ending' trail which undulates through gullies and winds in and out of the trees. The trail traverses the side of the hill, before dropping down towards Busquistar. Keep your eye out for GR markers for reassurance. After a while arrive at a junction in the trail.

6 Descent into Busquistar

Follow the GR left and begin your descent into Busquistar. The trail descends steeply at first, taking you round switchbacks, and through trees, before spitting you out just left of a wide open area. Follow the wide track to the left until you come across another GR marker. On a sharp left hand bend is the GR heading straight on, marked by the post. Follow the GR for more fun and games. After an old rickety bridge reach a wider track leading you down into Busquistar. Follow this downhill as it turns into concrete and reaches the main road.

7 Busquistar

Go right at the road and head out of Busquistar. A few hundred metres out of the village look out for what looks like a steep driveway heading up to the right. Take this and after 100m go left at a fork. Climb steeply and pass a building on your left. The trail narrows and levels out now, taking you between fields. At a building on your left and another fork, take the trail to your left to arrive at a concrete track above the main road. At the road turn right and pedal on up for about 1km to Portugos. Go as far as the 'Jamone's de Portugos'.

8 'Jamone's de Portugos'

Opposite 'Jamone's de Portugos' is a gap in the fence and a track leading down. This is the start of the next piece of trail which descends to the village of Atalbeitar, on a loosely surfaced windy track. The GR markings are pretty scarce here and because there are tracks coming in from all directions it is best to follow the clearer marker posts for the 'Ruta Medieval' until you reach the village.

9 Atalbeitar

At Atalbeitar follow the track into the village square and carry on through to the other side, and the road out. Continue uphill along the road towards Pitres for just under 1km. At the first right hand hairpin the GR carries straight ahead. Take this to go uphill at first. Soon it narrows and drops downhill towards the inside of the gully. Enjoy this while it lasts because it's a bit of a push out the other side. Continue steeply to Pitres. Follow the track through the streets to the main road.

10 Pitres

At the road turn right heading uphill. After a 300m and a speed bump take the left to Capilerilla. After 30m a road comes in from the right, stick left and carry on uphill as the tarmac gets steeper. At the village the road narrows, follow it underneath concrete roofing taking the first right immediately after. Climb steeply up through the narrow streets, take the first left, to bring you out the other side of the village and opposite the GR track.

11 Capilerilla

Follow the track rightwards as it climbs uphill next to a wall. It can get a bit confusing here with trails joining and splitting off in all directions. Head steeply up until you reach a wide open space between tracks. Take the main vehicle track straight up and then the first wide track that branches off left. Follow this, until you reach a chain across the track. Turn left onto the track and follow it as it gradually climbs to reach a big crossroads after 1km.

12 Crossroads

At the crossroads are hundreds of sections of concrete pipes. In-front the GR trail disappears downhill. Take this and after 500m arrive at the hairpin of a tarmac road next to a grafitted ruin. Follow the road right and uphill for 500m. Keep an eye out for a GR marker post and trails coming in from either side.

13 Trail marker post

Take a well deserved rest here before dropping in to the trail on the left, for the final descent into Bubion. Start off with a steep straight liner before tightening up and twisting left and right through the trees. The corners get faster again as you come out into the open and finally drop you down onto the road. Head straight across to find the trail again which is just left of the metal barrier. It suddenly gets a lot more technical from here on in as it takes you through tight rocky switchbacks.

Finally near its end the trail leads onto a cobbled path to take you down to the main road in Bubion and a finish right in the heart of the village.

bikefaX

22 Las Alpujarras

The Ruta Medieval

Summary

A little off the beaten track, the Ruta Medieval offers a change of scene, and in winter when there is snow lying on the high sierra, a welcome rise in temperature can be found on this side of the hills.

The route starts you off with some 'no messing' tight technical switchbacks to then mellow for a while, but still with plenty of interesting and narrow singletrack. The landscape en route is constantly changing from agricultrural to lunar and finally to the all too familiar by now rocky descents the Apujarras are renowned for.

The piece de resistance is a stunning finale down the steep slopes of El Fuerte, where warmed up and fully body armoured, you can relax, hang off the back and enjoy the drops.

Neiles 

Expert 

Hard 

800 m 

4 - 5 hrs 

Sierra Nevada Series Penibetica 

Getting there

The tiny village of Nieles is located on the eastern side of the Alpujarras. To get there go through Trevelez and follow the road round the other side of the gorge to a junction. Go left here towards Juviles. Just before Juviles turn right for Nieles.

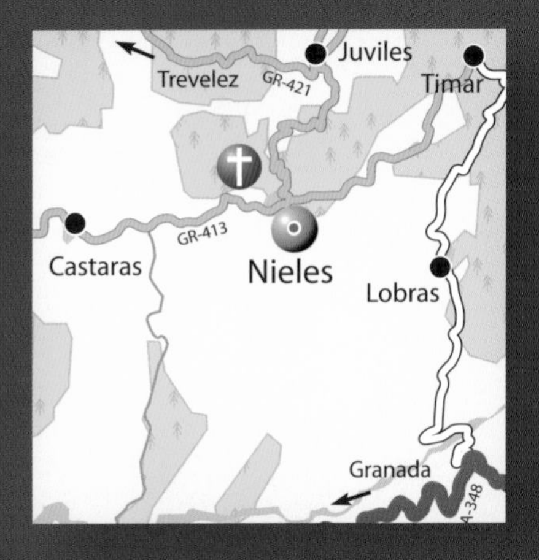

Start point

Park next to the church at the bottom end of the village.

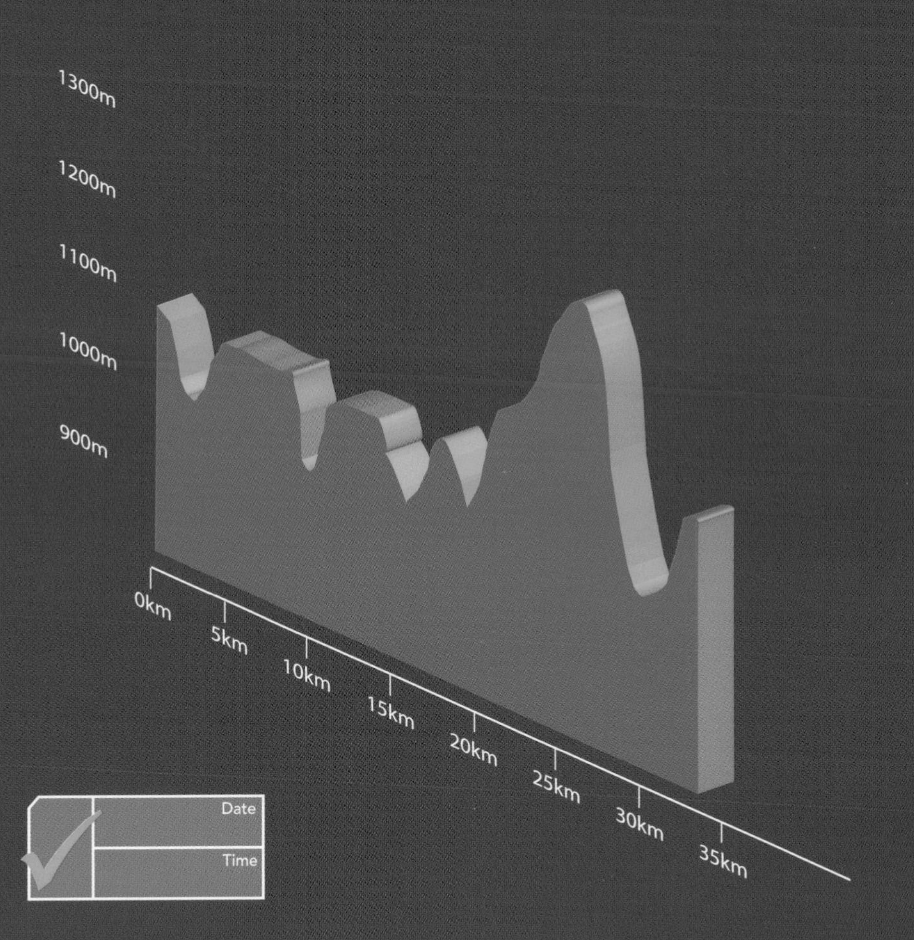

Date

Time

N
.1621
La Macaya
1500
1400
10
Alcutar
1200
1100
C-323
1191
Narila
Alto de
la Atalaya
11
12
.1255
Juviles
Cadiar
To Trevelez
El Fuerte
1304
Timar
.1154
13
9
3
4
5
.974
8
.1034
Nieles
Ruta Medieval
El Bombo
994
Cerro de
Lobrascon
1050
6
Lobras
1
2
GR7
Rio Guadalfeo
C-332
.901
To Orgiva
7
1km

Route description

Start

From the church, head back out of the village for just 50m, keeping your eyes peeled rightwards for a steep concrete path doubling back on itself. Follow this downwards. Occasional red and white markers for the GR142 confirm that you on the right path.

The path soon turns into steep twisty singletrack with the odd loose step; a real wakeup call at the start of the ride, but a great way to get going. Continue all the way down to a stream at the bottom of the ravine.

1 Stream

Cross the stream and follow markers diagonally rightwards to climb gently (for the most part) up the side of the hill, until you join up with a wide flat path – the Ruta Medieval.

2 Ruta Medieval

Turn left and follow the wide level path, passing several strange pipes and valves poking out of the ground. As you approach the end of the hill on your right, the path turns into track in front of a house. Follow the track leftwards.

3 Lunar landscape

Just around the corner from the house, the scenery suddenly turns into a weird lunar landscape with rain weathered silt piles in front of you. Here the track doubles back on itself, going rightwards and heading steeply up to a col.

4 Col

At the col, go over and down (red & white markers again), and ride through steep and deep ruts in the silt. Part way down the wider track, more of the same silty ruts appear on the left. Take these if you want more - you end up at the same end point as the track. Finish this section by dropping steeply into a stream crossing.

5 Stream

At the stream, the trail straight ahead looks horribly steep. Don't worry; this isn't the way out of the gully. Look to your right, and follow a very faint line of singletrack. This soon becomes a good dirt path rising around the side of the ravine. Although it's all rideable, it's not somewhere you would want to fall off.

At the end of the path, join the road and turn right towards the village of Lobras. Stop at a fuente (water fountain) on the right just as you enter the village.

6 Fuente

This is a good water fill up on a hot day. Just past the fuente, on the left, a wooden GR142 sign points you down the next section of trail. The trail starts wide and fast, narrowing to rutted intricate singletrack which rises and falls across the ridge line. At a circular stone platform, the trail appears to go cold. Go left and steeply down followed by a short steep push back up.

At the top of this twisty singletrack, a wide track heads right and takes you quickly down the crest of a ridge, heading onto the smaller left ridge where it splits. At the end of this a thrillingly steep and dusty descent deposits you at a wide open area with the inevitable stream at the bottom.

7 GR markers to Cadiar

At the bottom of the ridge, several GR markers

point in all sorts of directions. Go left following the GR7 to Cadiar. Again a good packed dirt path rises up the side of the hillside to a saddle and olive groves at the top, rideable all the way. The next section heading across and down from the col, still on the GR7, is a narrow rollercoaster of lovely singletrack weaving its way down to a wider track running alongside the river, and to the next village of Cadiar.

8 The Bridges of Cadiar

Double track leads you to the first green railing bridge to the south of Cadiar. Either cross this and follow the road to the right of the river to Cadiar, or more fun drop onto the track on the left of the river and follow this to the next green railing bridge, crossing a ford just before the second bridge to get up onto it. Cross the second bridge heading out of Cadiar in the direction of Timar.

9 Wide track climb upwards

The track leaving the second bridge from Cadiar soon heads upwards, passing a small house on the right and continuing on upwards. Follow this climb until you reach the first junction with a sign pointing leftwards to Timar. Take the right turn here and continue to head upwards.

Follow the track upwards, going round to the right of a small hill and then cutting back left, passing a small collection of houses, and continuing upwards climbing towards a cemetery (Cueva de los Pobres) and a small sports court on the side of the main road. All in all a steady 400m of climbing!

10 Road link to Juviles

Once on the main road, turn left to climb up at first, then descending into Juviles. Now for the best descent of the route! Just as you enter Juviles look out for a track heading off to the left just before a grand stone-built factory. A sign at the start of the track says 'Fuerte de Juviles'. This is the GR7 again, which is where the route is heading next.

11 GR7 towards Timar

Take the track down and follow it leftwards at the first t-junction to quickly descend, on a steep but wide track. Cross the small ford at the base of the track and climb steeply up, following this track as it narrows.

Keep following the red and white GR markers, and watch for where the track goes slightly leftwards (signposted 'Fuerte' right, GR straight on). Here, rather than heading up rightwards to the top of the El Fuerte, follow great singletrack down and up as it weaves up to a small rocky col before the best of the descent into Timar.

12 Singletrack heaven into Timar

From the rocky col continue to follow the GR7 down into Timar, with an excellent combination of rocky steps, switchbacks, and fast singletrack, an amazing section of trail to finish off the route – nearly! Either contemplate heading back up to do laps on this, or work your way through Timar, down and rightwards in the direction of Nieles.

13 Road link to Nieles

Head out of Timar and pick up the link road to Nieles (this new road is not marked on the maps). The road descends steeply down and then gives you one last hill to climb until you traverse quickly along the road back into Nieles. Take a left at the final junction and head down the road into the village.

Section 6

Lomas de Padul	23	XC / DH
Alto de Calar	24	XC
Fuente Teja	25	XC
Los Parapetes	26	XC
El Torro	27	XC / DH

Introduction

The Sierra Nevada stretches eastwards from Granada and contains some of the highest mountains in Spain. With Mulhacen at 3482m, sitting squarely and majestically in the middle of the range, there can be year round snow on the highest peaks.

Everything above 2000m is designated the Sierra Nevada National Park, and within the park mountain biking is only permitted on dirt tracks and is strictly controlled on the higher slopes. Lower down in the mountains though the riding is largely undiscovered, and on the fringe towns of Granada, such as Monachil and Padul, mountain bikers are taking over the abundant motocross trails and making them their own.

In the Sierra Nevada more great descents await, and many more are yet waiting to be discovered in this little ridden region. The riding varies from pure adrenalin satisfying descents such as the ride down from Los Parapetes or El Torro, to the more laid back but adventurous outings on the dirt trails of Alto de Calar.

Where to stay

At just 30km and 30 mins drive from Granada, the small village of Guejar Sierra is the best base for a trip to this area. Camping Las Lomas, just on the edge of the village, is a great spot to stay and also has log cabins for rent.

There are plenty of inexpensive places to rent in the area and a quick search on the web will come up with plenty of choices. Staying around Guejar Sierra is recommended for easy access to the rides, but you can also stay higher up the hill near the ski resort of Pradollano.

www.guejar-sierra-granada.co.uk
www.holidaylettings.co.uk/guejar-sierra
www.ownersdirect.co.uk/guejar-sierra.htm
www.campinglaslomas.com
www.nevadaactive.com

Food & drink

Staying this close to Granada it would be rude not to pop into town at least once for food. Tapas is a speciality in this city and you can get a free tapas (a small portion of whatever the house special happens to be) with virtually every beer. In the evenings the centre of town comes alive and there are great bars and restaurants to suit every taste.

Guejar Sierra is a popular tourist destination, and the tiny road alongside the Rio Genil abounds with quality restaurants. If you're staying at Camping Las Lomas, the terrace bar and restaurant here is good for feeding tired riding legs and has a good view of the fantastic 'El Torro' trail.

If you're self-catering, make sure you do your shopping before you leave Granada.

Bike shops & services

The biggest bike shop in the area is the excellent 'Semar Elite', near the city centre in Granada at San Anton. This huge chaotic shop stocks virtually everything. 'Sprinters' is a huge Decathlon style warehouse on the side of the motorway (exit 132) and Durcal has a small MTB shop off the main square at Plaza Suto.

Summary

The expansive forested hills of the Lomas de Padul hide a myriad small paths and trails, most of them not on any maps and all of them excellent sport to ride. The figure of eight route described here, is typical of the trails hereabouts; narrow, little ridden and dry as dust. Low down on the hillside on the open ground above the new housing developments, local mountain bikers and motocross riders have both created a network of tracks and you don't have to go far to find some fun. A bit of exploration here, will have you digging out trails all over the place.

Just along the road from Padul, in the neighbouring town of Durcal, is the only mountain bike shop for miles, and if it's jumps you want, then go and find the world class BMX track on the edge of the village.

Padul 

Expert 

Hard 

20km 

1000m 

3 - 4 hrs 

Padul 1026-IV

Getting there

Padul is located just off the motorway 30km south of Granada. To get there from the south and the Alpujarras, join the motorway (N323) in the direction of Granada. Leave the motorway at junction 144 for Padul.

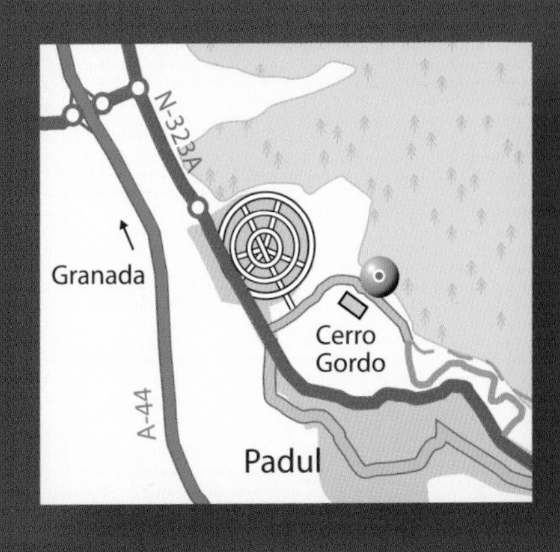

Start point

The route starts at the base of the forest on the north side of the town.

On leaving the motorway head into Padul on the Avenida de los Almendros. Just after passing a large collection of new houses on the left side of the road, you'll see a large garden centre. Go left here alongside the garden centre and follow the small road (the Calle de Gordo 2) up to the top of the small hill to a collection of factory buildings. Just beyond the factory find a place to park on the side of the road.

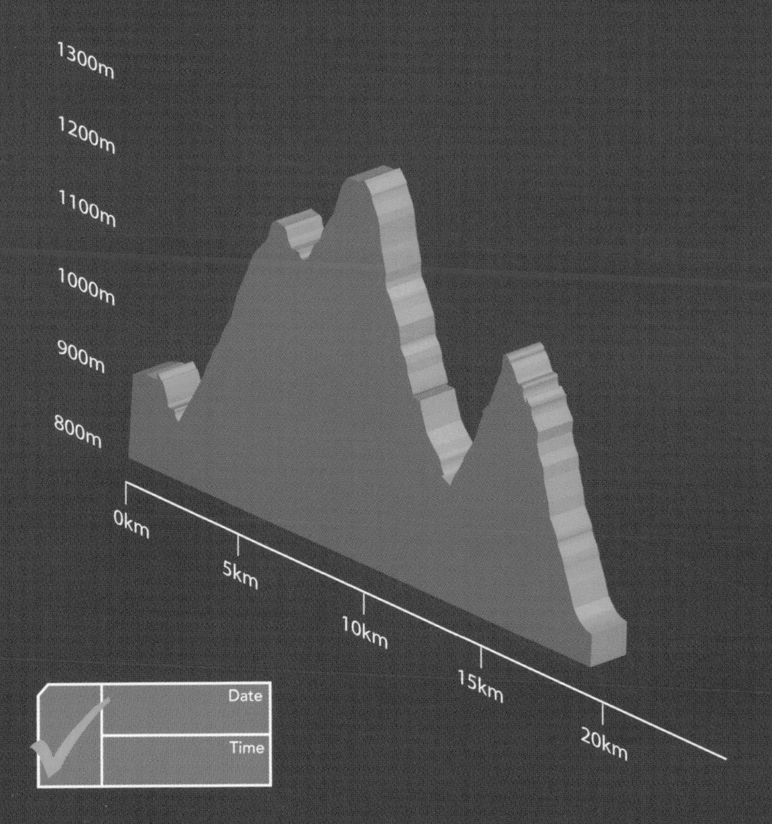

Date

Time

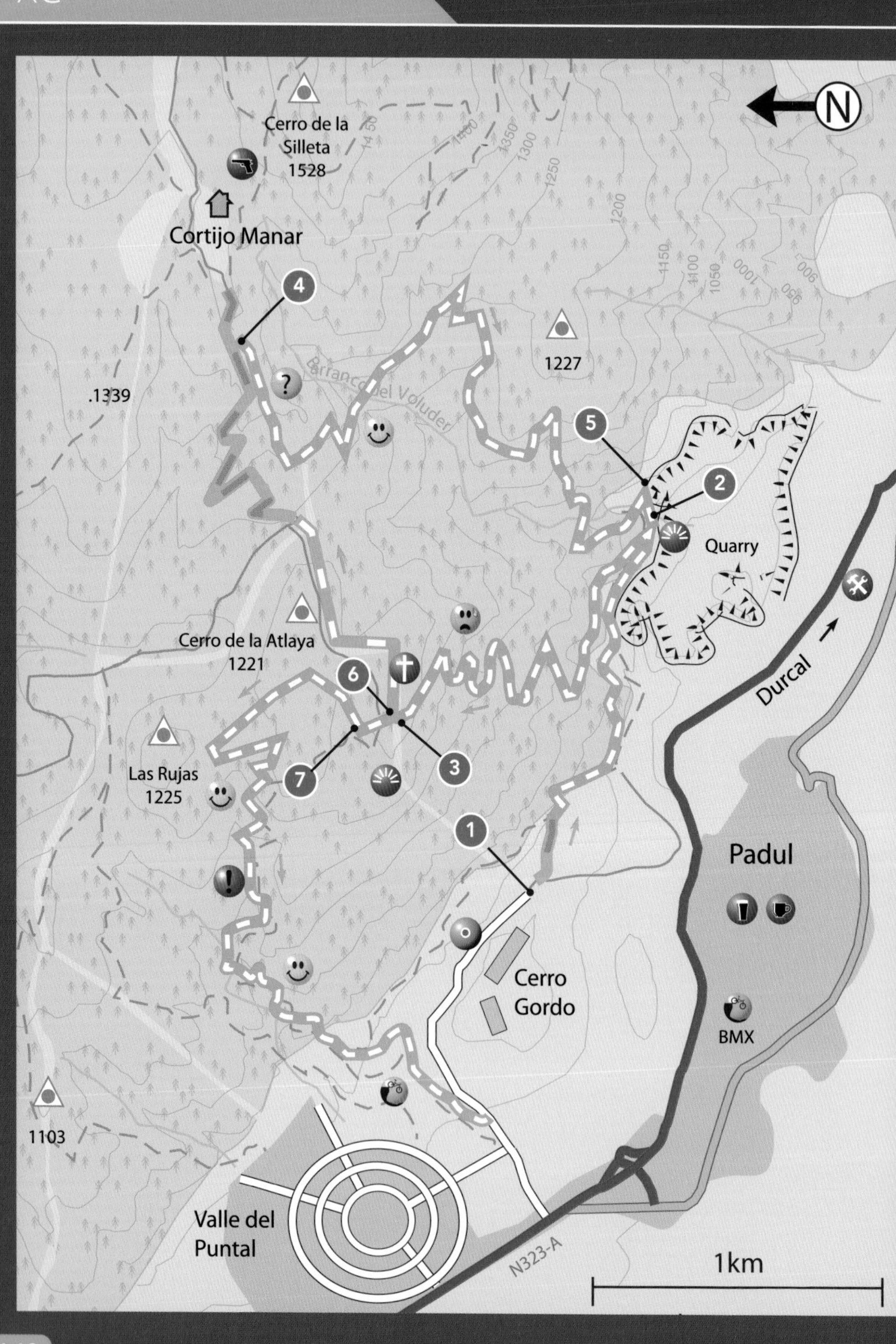

N
Cerro de la
Silleta
1528
Cortijo Manar
1400
1350
1300
1250
1200
1150
1100
1050
1000
950
900
4
1227
.1339
Barranco del Voluder
5
2
Quarry
Cerro de la Atlaya
1221
6
7
3
Las Rujas
1225
1
Durcal
Padul
Cerro
Gordo
BMX
1103
Valle del
Puntal
N323-A
1km

Route description

Start

Follow the tarmac road on from the factory. Rounding a corner take a track off left.

1 Dirt track

Follow the dirt track leftwards. After 500m the track bends sharply off to the right with singletrack heading off left. Follow the singletrack immediately goinh over a narrow stone bridge onto a well used trail. Pedal up this as far as a set of concrete steps. Arrive at a viewpoint overlooking the town, at a bend in the track with a trail coming in from the left.

2 Track/trail junction

Go left, engage a sane gear and begin plodding on up. Enjoy the views as you wind your way up the hill, watching out for some awkward switchbacks as you go. Finally arrive at a wide firebreak.

3 Firebreak

Go right and push or ride up the firebreak to the Cross. Pause for a moment of gawping at the views and then continue up the firebreak and down it to join a track.

At a big wide junction in tracks take the track heading straight uphill. Pedal up, rounding a few corners, keeping an eye out for a piece of single track off to the right almost heading back the way you have come (miss this and you'll arrive a large open field).

4 Singletrack

Padded up and ready to rock, begin heading down the narrow trail. Drop gradually and reach a split after 100m. Take the right-hand fork (left takes you to a viewpoint on a narrow ridge) and follow it as it twists its way through the bushes with tight, hard-packed gravel switchbacks. Here, trail feels hardly used by bike or walkers, this adds to the sense of adventure. Soon you drop into a dried out river bed. Pick the trail up again on the far side and finish with a short blast down to meet up with a track below and your earlier viewpoint.

5 Viewpoint

At the viewpoint, you will see the path you ascended earlier to the cross, unfortunately you are going to have to bite the bullet and ascend one more time.

Grind your way to the top again, see if you can get round every switchback this time.

6 Firebreak

When you reach the firebreak at the top, head straight over on a track leading into the forest. As the track levels out, look left to spot a thin trail disappearing into the trees. This has been marked by local riders with green spot rocks.

7 Final descent

The track sets off at a gentle gradient, slowly getting more and more technical and twisty. As the trail drops into a slightly steeper gradient with a series of deep motocross carved ruts, continue left as you start making your way around the hillside with some interesting rock features to tackle.

Before long the trail spits you out into the open where you will clearly see Padul and the factory you rode towards earlier in the day. Finish the short blast back down built jumps and berms to the road and make your way back up to your car.

Summary

The mountains above the small village of Guejar Sierra offer endless ridgelines to follow and the almost year round snows of the High Sierra making the area feel more alpine than Spanish.

Until very recently, the road was just a dirt track. Now it is a long but easy climb taking you out of the village up to the highest point possible in order to give back the maximum amount of descent in equal measure.

Like most spanish rides, there is the odd short lived bit of pushing to get you up to the top of the hill, but once up on the summit, the long snaking brown line of singletrack in front of you leaves no time for cursing. The descent starts here and keeps on going all the way back to Guejar Sierra. Ascending is both straightforward, and interesting and the descents, rocky and technical.

Guejar Sierra 

Expert 

Extreme 

18 km

1200 m 

3 - 5 hrs 

Sierra Nevada Penebetica 

Getting there

Guejar Sierra is situated just 22km east of Granada. From the direction of Granada and the motorway, take the A4026 to Pinos Genil. At Pinos go straight on to Guejar Sierra.

Start point

Parking is pretty limited in Guejar Sierra. There is space just below the Hotel Rural or park just before you enter the village at Camping Las Lomas where there is a great bar with a terrace for the end of the ride. Or if you want to save yourself a bit of the hill climb at the beginning of the day, drive up the hill and park at 'Camping Balderas' (1550m) and then volunteer someone to go and get the car at the end of the day!

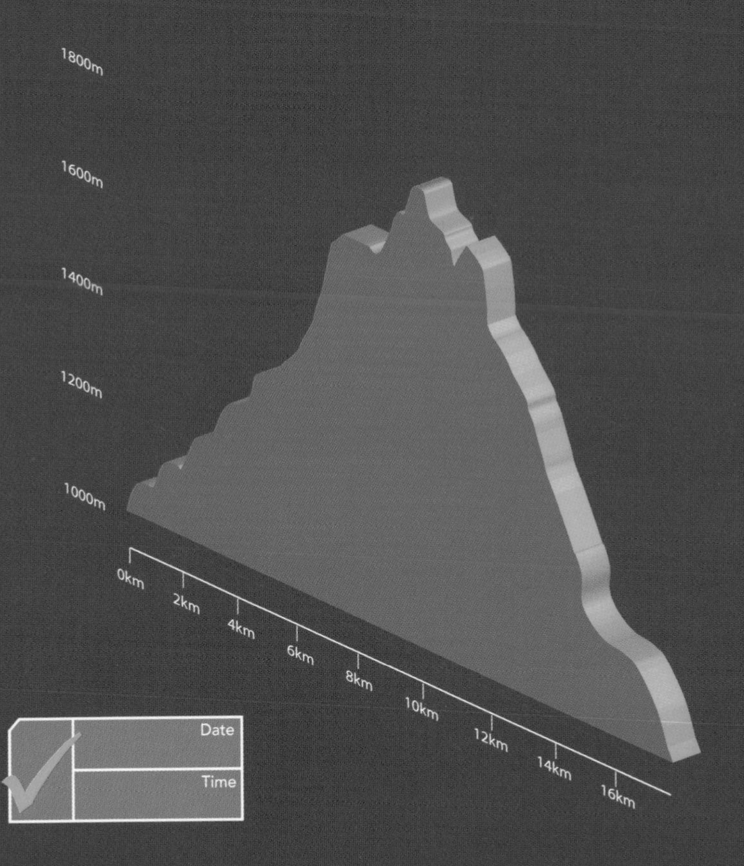

Date

Time

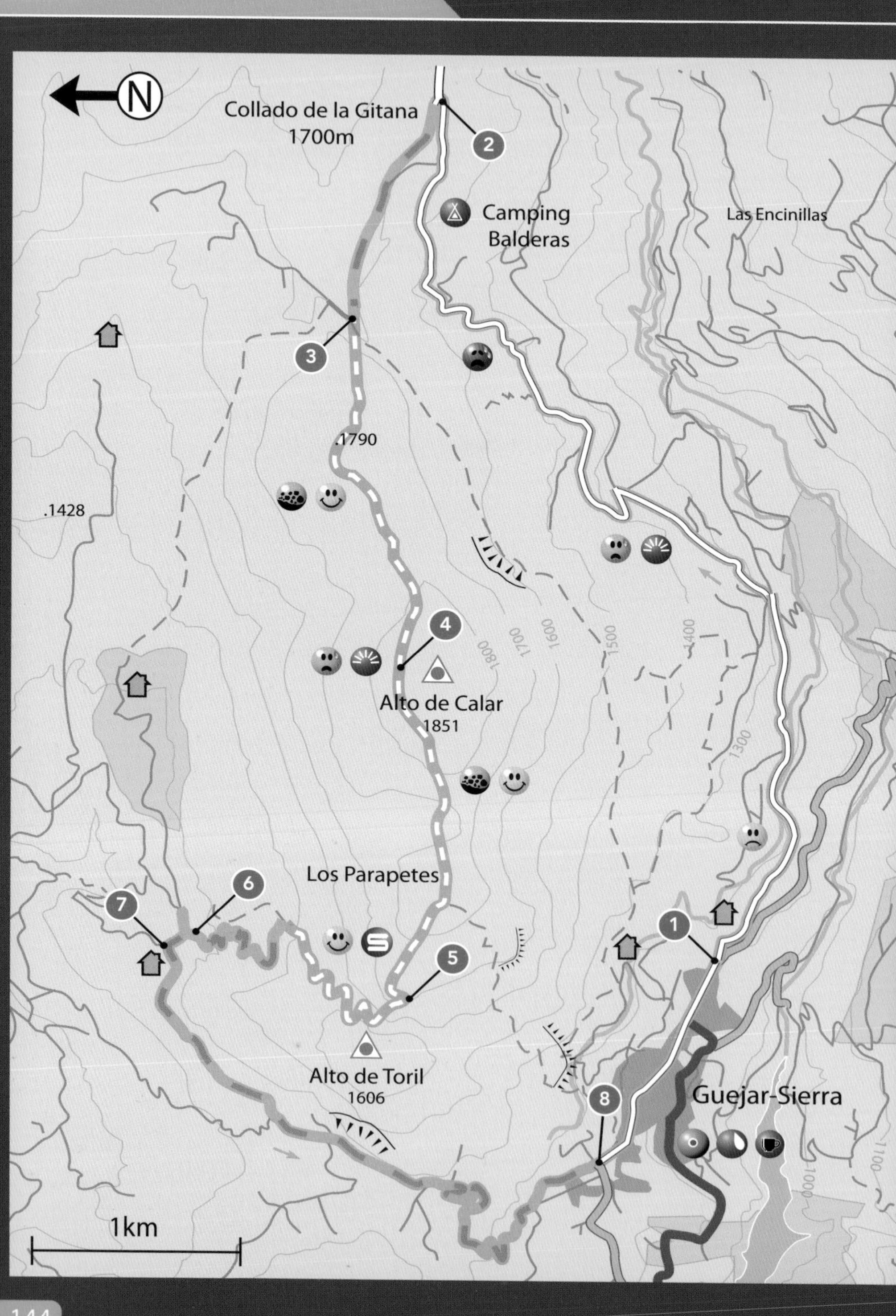
N
Collado de la Gitana
1700m
2
Camping
Balderas
Las Encinillas
3
.1790
.1428
4
Alto de Calar
1851
1800
1700
1600
1500
1400
1300
Los Parapetes
6
7
5
1
Alto de Toril
1606
8
Guejar-Sierra
1000
1100
1km

Route description

1 Road junction

Leave Guejar Sierra and just outside the village is a steep unsignposted tarmac road heading up left. A collection of wooden signboards at the start points upwards to 'Camping Cortijo Balderas'. Climb steadily up here and pass Camping Balderas on the right.

2 Dirt track

A kilometre after Camping Balderas a good dirt track cuts into the road at an angle on the left. Go up here to a wide flat col; the Collado de la Gitana, where a wooden sign points you in the direction of Cerro el Calar.

3 Track bend / Collado de la Gitana

From here you can see the path as a thin orange line making its way steadily up the hill. Apart from the odd rock step this is, in the main part rideable. Keep following the path all the way to the summit

4 Summit Alto de Calar 1878m

A wooden sign and a bunch of rocks declare that you have reached the top of the mountain. Having worked so hard to get here, it's worth staying a while and savouring the panoramic views. An excellent descent is about to begin and this is the time to pad up.

From the summit the descent looks gentle enough, but just over the brow things change rapidly and just as you start gaining speed the trail suddenly steepens. With a loose undersurface of small rocks and dust, it's easy to find yourself unexpectedly off line and in the bushes on the side. Keep your speed at the end for the small rise to Los Parapetes.

5 Los Parapetos

One tremendous section of descent over, have a wander round the old wartime bunkers of Los Parapetes and prepare for the next downward session. From here the trail continues over the rise and then drops steeply to the next col. Put your seat down and pads on, both are definitely advisable as this next section is steep, rocky and tight. An awesome section of trail which will have you working for every turn.

6 Col Alto del Toril

At the col the trail continues rightwards, snaking its way consistently backwards and forwards across the small valley making the most of the tight space available. As you continue your descent the track widens out and speeds up, following an old motocross trail to the big dirt track at the bottom.

7 Dirt track

The technical stuff over, you can put the seat back up and take off the pads. Might as well let some of that Spanish sun get to your legs after all.

Turn left at the track and follow around to a col above the Guejar Sierra Valley. Keep heading down from here with lots of cheeky singletrack options to cut off the corners.

8 Fuente de la Teja

Just after the fuente come into a small square where there is a more appetising looking water fountain on the left. Go left out of the square and follow your nose leftwards through narrow streets to the main square of Guejar Sierra, where there are plenty of cafés. Or turn right if you've left your car at Camping Las Lomas.

bikefaX

25 Sierra Nevada Fuente Teja

Summary

For those who would rather go around the mountain rather than up and over it, the Fuente Teja circuit offers the benefits of a very sweet flowing descent on fast earthy singletrack in return for just one short grunt of a climb.

An easy start up a dirt track is followed by a somewhat ruthless climb to the Collado de la Gitana. At the col gasp at the stupendous views of the Sierra Nevada's highest peaks with their almost year round snow, and then fly down towards the tiny buildings of Guejar Sierra in the distance.

A brilliant descent through wild pinnacles and lumpy limestone is interspersed with smooth non technical singletrack. There are great views throughout and the ride conveniently finishes right back at the square where you started from.

Guejar Sierra

Expert

Hard

3

17 km

800 m

3 - 4 hrs

Sierra Nevada Penebetica

Getting there

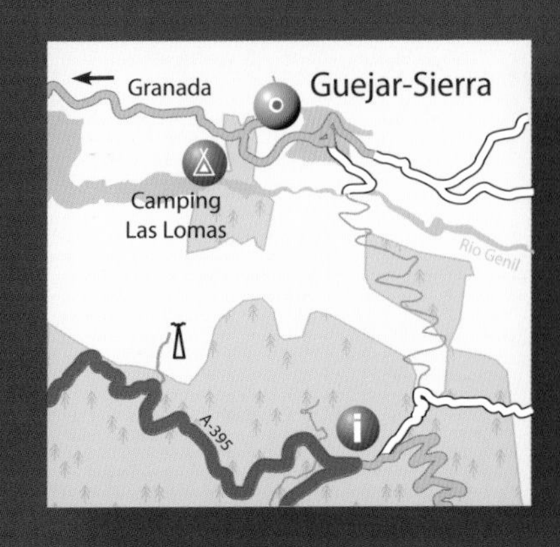

Guejar Sierra is situated just 22km east of Granada. From the direction of Granada and the motorway, take the A4026 to Pinos Genil. At Pinos go straight on to Guejar Sierra.

Start point

Just before you enter Guejar Sierra from the direction of Granada, pass the entrance to 'Camping Las Lomas' on the right. 100m after this is a small road going uphill on the left (signposted 'Cementerio Barrio Alto'). Take this and follow the road to a small square with a water fountain on the right. Park here.

Start

Head up the track on the top left of the square, going in the direction of the Fuente de la Teja. At the fuente, continue straight on up the track, as it zigzags onwards and upwards.

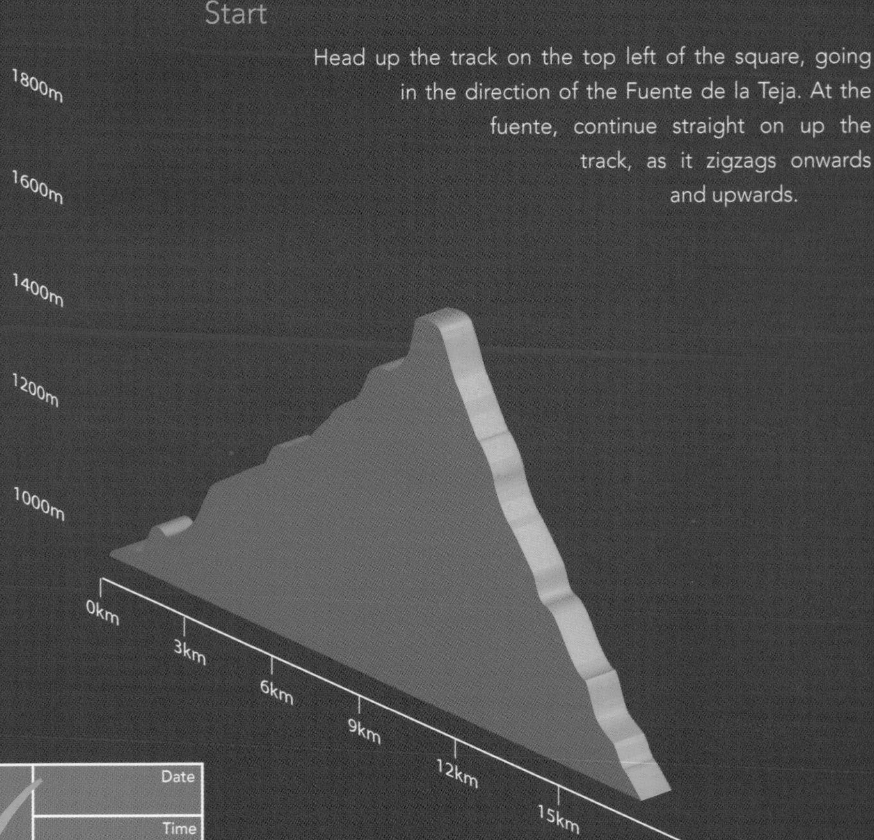

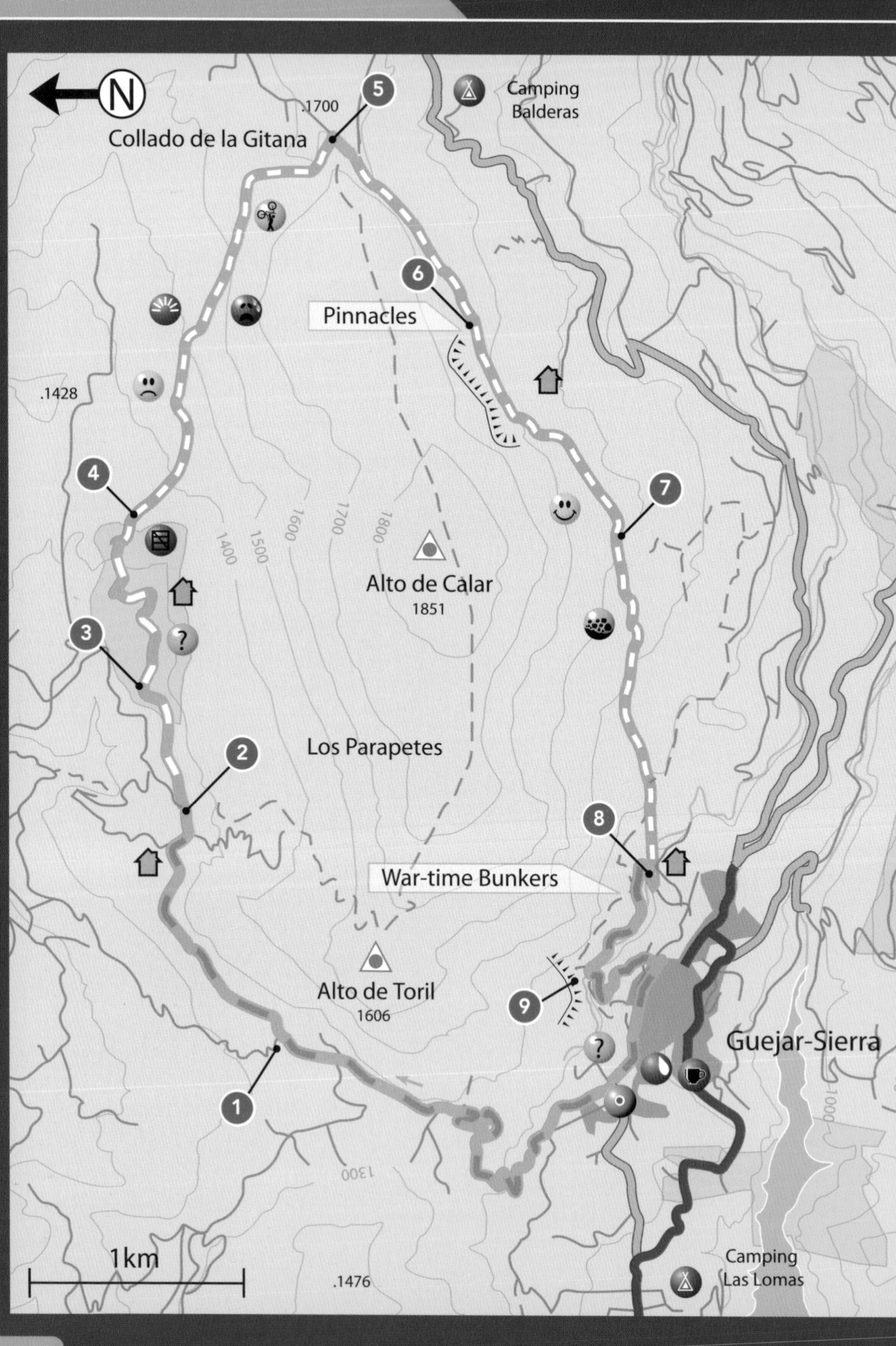

N
5
.1700
Collado de la Gitana
Camping
Balderas
6
Pinnacles
.1428
4
7
1400
1500
1600
1700
1800
Alto de Calar
1851
3
2
Los Parapetes
8
War-time Bunkers
Alto de Toril
1606
9
Guejar-Sierra
1
1300
1100
1000
1km
.1476
Camping
Las Lomas

Route description

1 Fork in track

Take a quick breather as the track heads downwards to a fork in the track. Go straight on and pass a white house on the left. Shortly afterwards you see the descent from Alto de Calar coming down from a col on the right. Continue straight on to another fork.

2 Fork in track

Take the righthand branch of the fork and peddle along a wide cart track through trees to arrive at a ramshackle house.

3 Cortijo

Go round to the left behind the house and up a steep rise to a field. The trail goes cold here for a while but soon picks up again. Follow the vague line through gorse and scrub rightwards from the house heading for a fence.

4 Makeshift gate

Go through the gate and follow the obvious path as it traverses up the mountain side. Depending on the size of your thighs there could well be a little pushing here and there. Still it's a pretty chilled out place to be and not much more than 15 minutes of pushing will see you over the worst of it. When the trail starts to ease off, get back in the saddle to go over one last rise and along earthy singletrack to arrive at a wide dirt track and a col.

5 Collado de La Gitana 1700m

Arrive at a wide track at a col where a wooden sign points right to the summit of Alto de Calar. From the col a series of trails braid their way along the left hand (southern) flank of the mountain. Head along any one of these, to join the main line at a fence.

6 Crazy pinnacles

Flowing earthy riding brings you to an area below high rusty cliffs where mad pinnacles of rock provide a photogenic foreground and the mountains as the holiday snap backdrop. Ride between the mad pinnacles of rock and continue on for some very smooth riding.

7 Limestone pavement

The pavement offers tricky riding. Look for the worn orange weathering on the rocks where the line of least resistance is to be found. Once through the rocks the trail does a bit of a wiggle rightwards, and then picks up speed on a fast (but loose) descent to a farm.

8 Track

After a brilliant descent, join a track near a farm and head downhill initially, and then right past a small quarry, now a collection of animal sheds. Ride along as far as an old wartime bunker on the right. Here the track splits into three. Take the middle track to pass the bunker. Now the track gets steep and loose as you descend underneath sandy cliffs. A small rise exits you from the cliffs, and places you at the start of olive groves above the village.

9 Sandy cliffs

Head straight on, following a vague line, as a collection of thin trails cross and re-cross each other over a ridge line to finally drop you onto a track by a pool and a small cliff. Follow a concrete track to arrive at the Fuente de la Teja and its multiple fountains. More appetising water is however, to be found back at the square.

Summary

A slice of some of the very best riding on this side of the Sierra Nevada, the Los Parapetes trail begins its descent with a fast earthy ride around the side of the hill and finishes with an all out testing and exhilarating switchback frenzy. From the Parapetes, a collection of wartime bunkers and lookout posts, the trail switchbacks mercilessly down the hillside above the cliffs.

The start, as with so many Spanish rides, is a long climb up and out of the valley. But the newly surfaced tarmac road up to the Collado de Alguacil, offers an easy ascent and a chance to appreciate the grandeur of the snowy mountains of the Sierra Nevada, with Mulhacen the highest peak in Spain at a mighty 3482m in altitude, right in front of you as you climb up.

Guejar Sierra 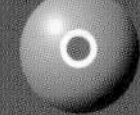

Epic 

Extreme 

18 km 

960 m 

5 hrs 

Sierra Nevada
Series Penibetica 

Getting there

Guejar Sierra is situated just 22km east of Granada. From the direction of Granada and the motorway, take the A4026 to Pinos Genil. At Pinos go straight on to Guejar Sierra.

Start point

Find a parking space on the edge of Guejar Sierra and head out of town in the direction of the Rio Genil. Just a couple of hundred metres outside the village is a steep unsignposted tarmac road heading up left. A collection of wooden signboards at the start points upwards to 'Camping Cortijo Balderas' (if you like your holidays remote, this is a good place to stay).

Alternatively get someone to drive you to the top of the road and the Collado de la Alguacil, and just head on down.

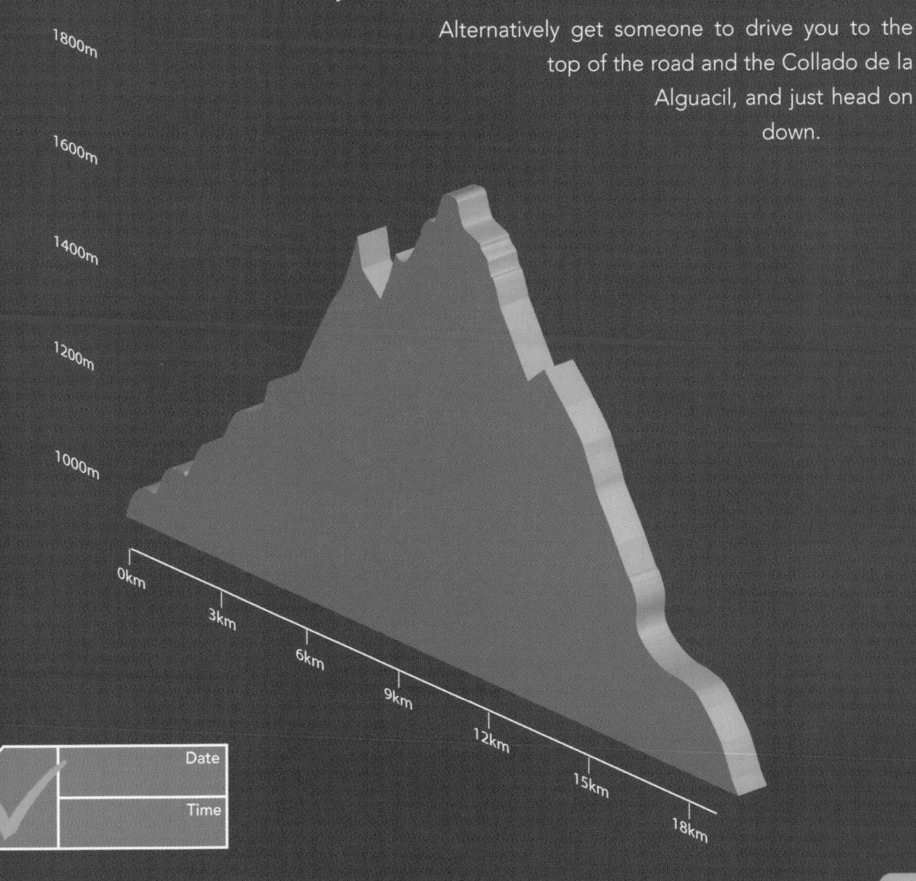

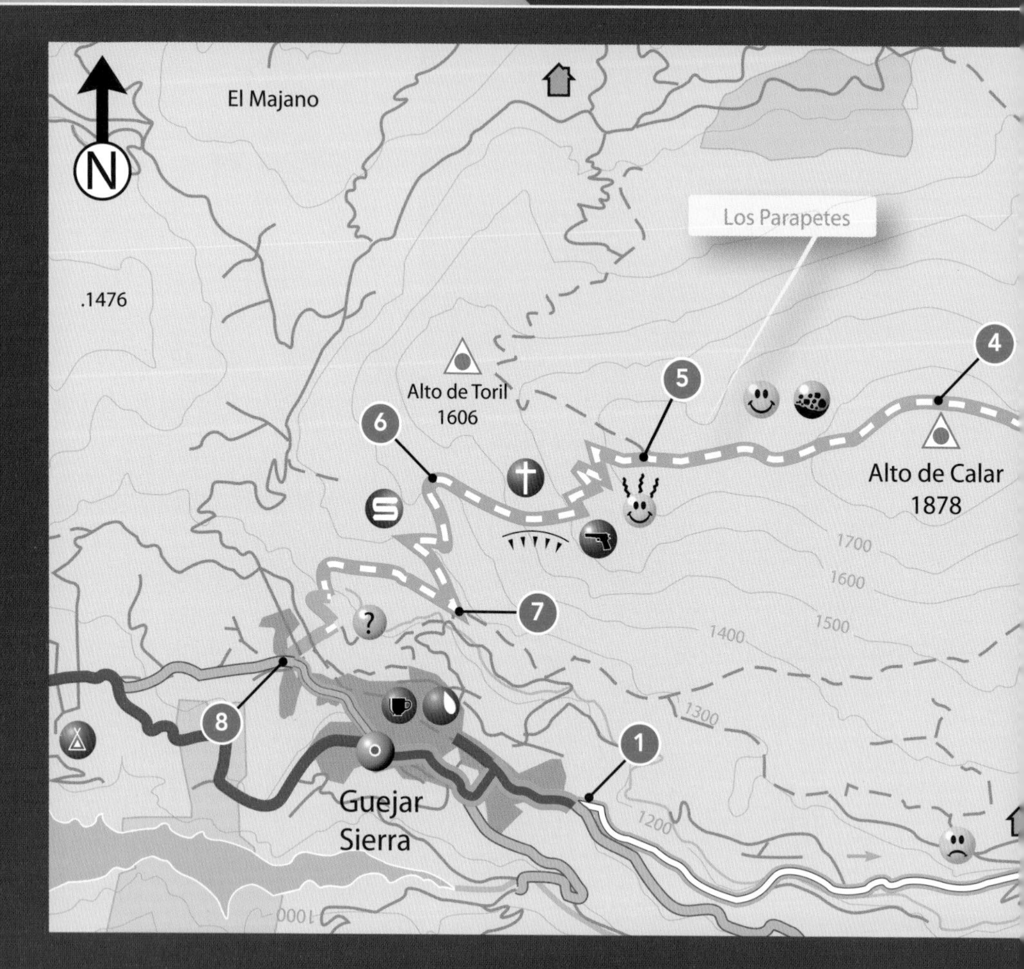

Route description

1 Road junction

Until recently this was a dirt track, now it is a newly surfaced smooth tarmac road. Simply follow this without deviation, passing 'Camping Balderas' about half way up on the right, to reach the top of the pass and a wide flat parking area, where the tarmac mysteriously ends.

Roadies will love this climb. And in fact Spanish road riders do too; they just ride all the way to the top from Granada, and blast right back down.

2 Collado de Alguacil 1880m

At the top of the hill, the road turns into track and this great viewpoint is a chance to spy out some of the as yet undocumented riding opportunities in the next valleys.

As you look back down the way you have just come, there is a wide dirt track on the right. This is the start of some great singletrack. Take the rutted track and follow it as it narrows towards a small col.

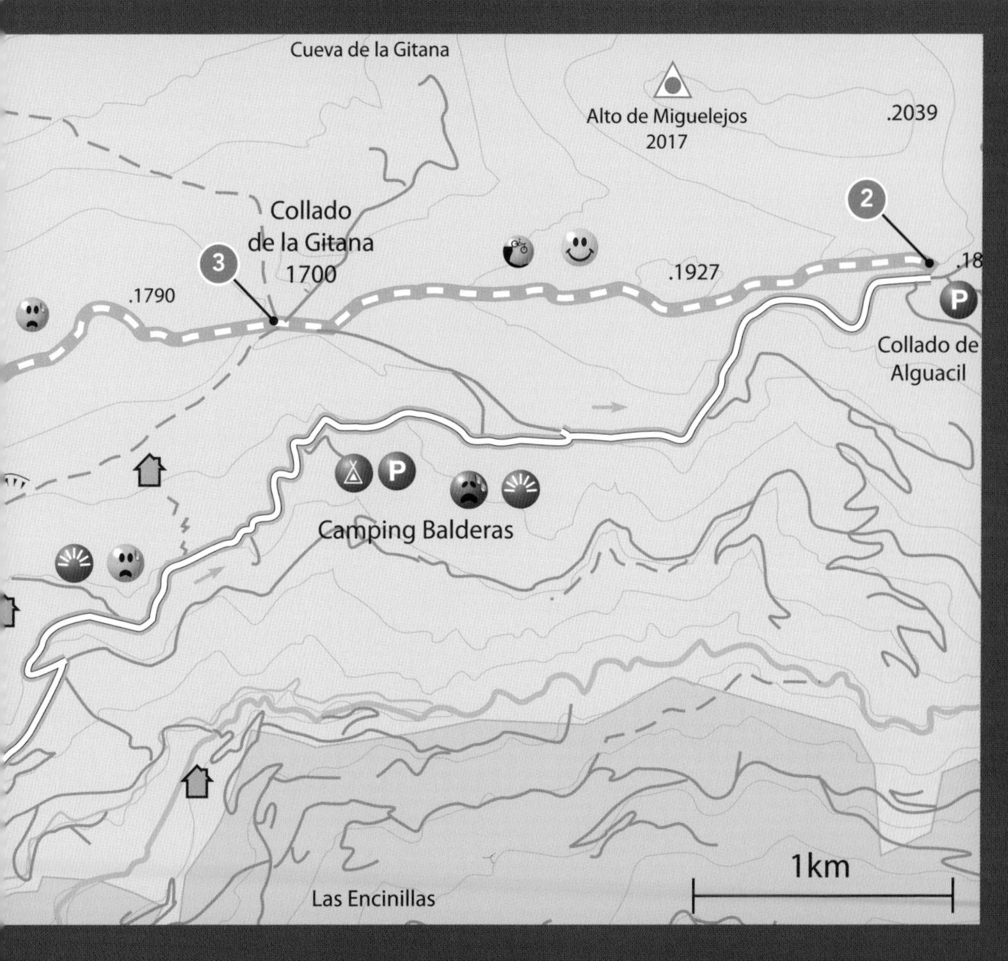

At the col, the trail drops steeply down loose stony ground, with some mild switchbacks to warm you up for the main event later. Lower down the trail changes its character as you pick up speed on easier angled terrain, and with a few jumps opportunities drops you onto the track above Camping Balderas.

Turn right here and ride for 200metres to a large righthand bend in the track at another broad col.

3 Collado de La Gitana 1700m

At the col a wooden sign points right to the summit of Cerro el Calar.

From here you can see the path as a thin orange line making its way steadily up the hill. Apart from the odd rock step, this section is in the main part rideable. After just a few hundred metres the path levels as you come to another small col. Ride along here, heading rightwards towards a wooden post.

Keep heading uphill (leftwards), the summit isn't far away. Ride as much as you can and then a final push through rocks for about 10 minutes has you at the summit.

4 Summit Alto de Calar 1878m

If you didn't allready know it, a wooden sign declares that you have reached the top of the mountain. From here, an excellent 360 degree panarama allows you the an opportunity to plan your next few days riding. And once this has been done a stunning descent is about to commence. This is the time to pad up. Dont be deceived by the seemingly innocent start to the descent as just as soon as you are over the brow, things change rapidly. With small loose rocks littering the trail, you really need to hang loose and float to have any chance of holding your line.

5 Los Parapetes

The descent from the summit of Alto Calar was just the warm up and before you head down again, take a wander around the old wartime bunkers and lookout posts of Los Parapetes.

If you haven't already put your seat down and pads on, then both are definitely advisable. The next section is technical and tight, getting more and more feisty, the further you descend.

To find the start of the next descent wander over to the gun emplacements on the south side of the hill and you'll see the clean sweep of the trail heading towards what looks like the very edge of the cliffs. Just before it goes over the edge, the trail takes a sharp right-hander and then makes its way steadily down. Keep your eyes open as this section ends at a particularly tight switchback right above a very steep cliff. From here more lively riding with a few short sections of real brain teasing steps bring you to a vantage point overlooking a perfectly carved section of trail and the 'Valley of the Switchbacks'.

6 'Valley of the Switchbacks'

A flying start into the valley seems to be the obvious course of action, but take care as every corner on this section is loose and dusty and wants to throw you straight off line. At the bottom of this brilliant section of riding you'll be panting, grinning and exhausted all at once.

At the end of all this the trail becomes a little difficult to follow. The most obvious line takes you left, and you're bound to end up going this way at first, everyone does, but eventually you'll locate the way rightwards. Once on track again, the path leads down through the lower slopes of the hill to join a wide track.

7 Track

Follow the track down past a water repository to join the road at Fuente de la Teja. A little caution here with speed as some of the drainage channels across the track can have you off in a second.

8 Fuente Teja

Water is available here, or just another 50 m further is a rather more appetising water fountain in the small village square. To get back to your car, go through the square taking the road on the bottom left of the square.

In Guejar Sierra (depending on the time of day) there are plenty of bars to quench your thirst. If you do hit the square at Siesta time and everything is closed, go out of town rightwards and head for the large 'Hotel Rural', which despite looking pretty posh has a nice terrace bar at the back and is quite happy to see cyclists.

bikefax

El Torro

27 Sierra Nevada

Summary

A five star route and something of a hidden gem. An unlikely start from the enormous cutout of 'El Torro' sneaks you onto the steep slopes above the reservoir and the Genil Valley, to then throw you down one switchback after another, through woods, rock, scree and finally orchards.

So discreet is the start of this route that you'd never find the trail without a little help, but once on it, the route finding is nothing but straightforward. Think of your fitness on the way up, enjoy coffee and the views at one of many bars on the ski road, and then set dial to smile zone, 'cos this is one route you'll definitely be back for, maybe even begging a lift second time round to take you straight to the top.

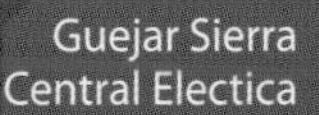
Guejar Sierra
Central Electica 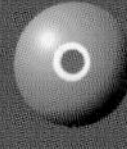

Expert 

Hard 

11 km 

600 m 

3 - 4 hrs 

Sierra Nevada
Series Penibetica 

Getting there

From the direction of Granada head into the village of Guejar Sierra and follow the one way system rightwards (following signs for the Rio Genil). Opposite the police station and as the one way system turns uphill, is a small road forking off to the right. Follow this down to the river and park at a large parking bay next to the bridge.

Start point

Start form the Rio Genil Central Electrica Substation below the village.

If you can find yourself a lift you can do this ride as a DH trip, as it's pure downhill all the way from El Torro.

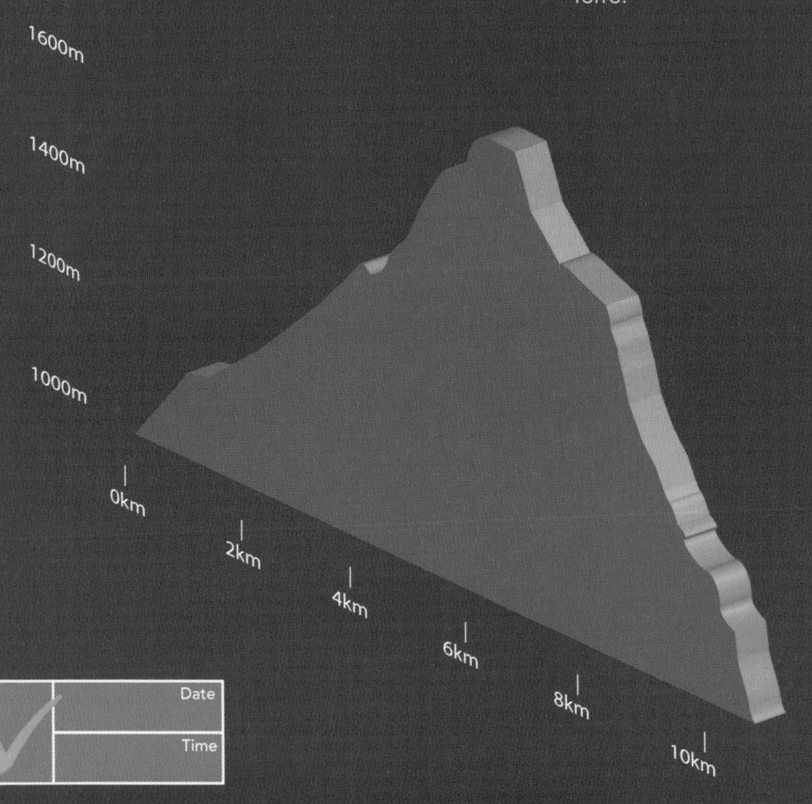

Date

Time

Route description

Start

Cross over the bridge from the Guejar Sierra side towards the 'Central Electrica' sub-station on the opposite side. Briefly follow the tarmac as it sweeps around to the right. The tarmac only lasts for about 100m before reaching a wide open dirt road. Follow this leftwards around a hairpin and begin your ascent.

1 Dirt road

Once on the dirt road, life is pretty straight forward, just keep winding your way up the main track around a series of steep hairpins. Ignore any tracks off to either side, and generally it is quite easy to distinguish the main track from more minor ones, so you shouldn't have to worry about getting lost just yet.

The gradient eases after a while and is just a steady plod, so choose a suitable gear, sit back and enjoy the view. There is one left hand junction about 2/3rds of the way up (1380m) that could confuse you, forget this though and continue rightwards underneath a high wall (on your left). Before long you will find yourself at a tarmac road.

2 Tarmac road

It's probably wise to take a breather here because it's not quite over yet. Turn right onto the road and carry on for 2km (looking out for the Morzine style 'red bubble' cablecar, strung from the trees). The hill continues at a gentle gradient until you reach a more major road.

Turn right onto this and head downhill for a couple of hundred metres until you hit an even bigger road. This is the main road from Granada to the ski resort at Pradollano.

Turn right and big ring it as you fly downhill overtaking cars. Keep your eye out for the big black bull 'El Torro Osborne' on the horizon, because this is where you are heading. It's along this section of tarmac that all the cafes and bars are located providing the perfect opportunity to recover from the climb.

After refreshments at the hostelry of your choice, blast down the road for a couple of kilometres, watching out for the dirt track off right leading to the bull itself and a large communications mast on a rocky ridge.

3 El Torro

Before you head down, get the obligatory family album shots of you all leaning against (a very anatomically correct) El Torro himself. And then if you've got time it's well worth an excursion up to the mast, where just beyond a small path allows you to scramble up onto the ridge. From here look down to the track leftwards and try to scan for the faint brown trail and small cairn that is the start of the singletrack.

Having spotted your trail head back on yourself towards the road and cut down to the lower track on your right. Follow this for around 500m gently downhill until it levels out. Look out for the vague head of the singletrack descent on your right. You may have trouble finding it at first, but have a little poke about and you will come across it. There is a small cairn at the trail head, but is easily missed amongst the hundreds of rocks strewn about.

Once you've found the start of the track head straight down. It's a lot steeper than it looked from above and has you perked up and concentrating hard as it dives into the trees. From now on it's a combination of steep, loose

N
Haza del Panizo
Cable Car
Rio Genil
Guejar-Sierra
Central Electrica
Los Alamos
Castanar de
Guejar-Sierra
To Ski
Resort
Petrol Station
Cerro del Monte
1612
A395
El Torro
.1884
Cerro del Castillo
1255
Embalse de Canales
Pico de la Lastra
To Granada
1km
1000
1100
1200
1300
1400
1500
1600
1700
1
2
3
4
5

switchbacks and fast straight liners – you'll love it. Before long, exit briefly from the trees into a rocky open area with spectacular views and a chance to check out some of the trails on Alto de Calar.

From here it's once again back into the trees where the gradient gets more manageable, but keep your wits about you still, for those large, baby head sized rocks lying about can come at you with no warning whatsoever.

4 Col

Finally leave the trees behind as you drop into a wide flat col in front of the iron cross sitting atop Cerro del Castillo. At the col notice a little wooden signpost which points (slightly misleadingly) left towards Guejar Sierra. In actual fact look over the edge of the col to your right and you should see the trail heading downwards underneath you.

Follow the path as it descends into the wide gully beneath you. Soon the path drops into some steep technical rock switchbacks before rounding a corner and heading across the stream, and the far side of the gully.

A fast and flowy piece of trail follows next, and just as you reach a piece of plastic pipe buried in the ground the trail ducks off left and through a tiny homemade gate.

A few more tight switchbacks immediately after this keeps you on your toes. Get it wrong and you'll be straight over a cliff!

The cliff safely negotiated carry on along a fast smooth path along blossoming groves of almond trees to reach a dirt road.

5 Dirt track

Blast back down the track, heading for the river. A short climb brings you to a section of tarmac you should recognise from the beginning of your climb. Go left to the bridge and your car.

Routes by grade

XC

Thanks & acknowledgements

Big thanks to so many people for riding with us, providing inspiration and for sheltering us and fixing our bikes along the way. Thanks to riders Jim Savege, Neil Halcrow, Matt Barnicott and Sue Peyton for many an enjoyable adventure; Seasonally Unadjusted, Switchbacks, Freeride Spain, Sierra Active and Trailrider Spain for inspiration and trail beta; Roy Hunt for letting us hang out in his flat in Padul on a cold rainy weekend, John and Christine at Finca la Campana El Chorro and Tina Emmott at Buena Vista for their excellent accommodation; thanks to Kona for the ever so versatile Dawg, and to Continental and Hope for the essential bits of kit.

Photographs:

Sue Savege. Additional photographs: Jim deBank, SeasonallyUNadjusted (pages: 9, 24, 38, 44, 45, 50, 58, 62, 68, 81, 85, 88, 92); Matt Barnicott (pages 123, 142, 150); Neil Halcrow (back cover).